KNOWLEDGE CAPITAL AND THE "NEW ECONOMY"

Firm Size, Performance And Network Production

Economics of Science, Technology and Innovation

VOLUME 20

Series Editors
Cristiano Antonelli, *University of Torino, Italy*
Bo Carlsson, *Case Western Reserve University, U.S.A.*

The titles published in this series are listed at the end of this volume.

KNOWLEDGE CAPITAL AND THE "NEW ECONOMY"

Firm Size, Performance And Network Production

by

Pontus Braunerhjelm
The Research Institute of Industrial Economics (IUI)
Stockholm, Sweden

KLUWER ACADEMIC PUBLISHERS
Boston / Dordrecht / London

Distributors for North, Central and South America:
Kluwer Academic Publishers
101 Philip Drive
Assinippi Park
Norwell, Massachusetts 02061 USA
Telephone (781) 871-6600
Fax (781) 871-6528
E-Mail <kluwer@wkap.com>

Distributors for all other countries:
Kluwer Academic Publishers Group
Distribution Centre
Post Office Box 322
3300 AH Dordrecht, THE NETHERLANDS
Telephone 31 78 6392 392
Fax 31 78 6546 474
E-Mail <services@wkap.nl>

 Electronic Services <http://www.wkap.nl>

Library of Congress Cataloging-in-Publication Data

Braunerhjelm, Pontus.
    Knowledge capital and the "new economy" : firm size, performance, and network
production / by Pontus Braunerhjelm.
        p. cm. -- (Economics of science, technology, and innovation ; v.20)
    "Part of the book's contents have also been presented as a doctoral thesis,
    defended in 1999 at Jönköping International Business School"--P..
    Includes bibliographical references and index.
    ISBN 0-7923-7801-6 (alk paper)
        1. Intellectual capital. 2. Industries--Size. 3. Production (Economic theory)
    I. Title. II. Series.

    HD53 .B72 2000
    338.5--dc21   00-023126

Printed on acid-free paper.

Printed in the United States of America

CONTENTS

ACKNOWLEDGEMENT

Different features associated with the "new economy" have recently emerged as one of today's most topical issues. In the public debate, as well as among academic researchers, increasing attention has been paid to the driving forces behind the mechanism of the "new economy". In particular, from a microeconomic point of view, the role of firm size, knowledge and cluster production has been stressed. This book focuses on these three particular components, rather than on presenting a full-fledged analysis of the new economy. Part of the book's contents have also been presented as a doctoral thesis, defended in 1999 at Jönköping International Business School.

Traditional ways of organizing industrial production have undergone dramatic and rapid changes during the last decades. Vertically integrated firms and Tayloristic structures have increasingly been replaced by organizations characterized by networks, clusters, and other informal types of cooperation between economic agents that is founded on mutual trust and interdependence. Such reorganization of industrial production opens new opportunities for small and medium-sized firms, but also challenges these firms' abilities to respond to a novel production environment. In particular, the internationalization of production that emanates from the dismantling of trade and investment barriers, in addition to advances in information technology, will stiffen competition in previously sheltered markets. Differences in prices and qualities will become more transparent, and the prospects for firms that fail to cope with these new conditions and requirements are bleak. Hence, a continuous upgrading of the firms' knowledge capital in terms of R&D capacity, marketing knowledge, and a skilled workforce will become crucial ingredients for firms to remain competitive, irrespective of size.

Most of the research work has been accomplished while I was associated with the IUI (The Research Institute of Industrial Economics) in Stockholm. IUI has a long tradition in this field, originating in Professor Erik Dahmén's seminal contributions to industrial organization and industrial dynamics in the early 1950s. Special thanks to IUI colleagues for commenting on an earlier version of this manuscript, particularly Erik Mellander and Roger Svensson. I am also grateful to Professors Magnus Blomström, Bo Carlsson, Gunnar Eliasson and Börje Johansson for commenting on different parts of the book. Finally, Per Thulin has provided excellent assistance with part of the empirical work, and Elisabeth Gustafsson helped to turn the different chapters into a coherent manuscript. For part of the work, generous financial support has been provided by the Marianne and Marcus Wallenberg Foundation and The Swedish National Board for Industrial and Technical Development (NUTEK).

Chapter 1

INTRODUCTION

1.1 Background

The concept of the "new economy" has recently emerged as a buzzword for policy makers all around the globe. In particular, its proponents claim that inflation is extinct because of increased competitive pressure emanating from advances in information technology (IT) and the deregulation of national as well as international markets. Simultaneously, the IT revolution helps to boost productivity and diffuse knowledge to firms that are linked in real or virtual networks. The fanatics see no limits to this development; however, they also claim that, for the firm, it is a matter of adapting to the new situation or dying.

No doubt the organization of industrial production has undergone considerable changes during the last couples of decades. In particular, decentralization, or downsizing, and internationalization have been two conspicuous features of the organization of industrial activity, despite the recent "megamerger" mania. These trends seem to interact and reinforce each other as competition sharpens between firms. This development also carries important repercussions for the operations of small and medium-sized firms (SMEs). It is the latter microeconomic aspects that are considered in the present book, rather than the macroeconomic issues. That is, we focus on the role attributed to knowledge, firm size and networks in the "new economy".

One aspect of decentralization is that, increasingly, production tends to be organized in complex networks, clusters and technological systems, which opens new opportunities from SMEs. Such networks can comprise an impressive number of firms and also stretch over several countries, or even continents. But they may also induce agglomeration into narrow geographically concentrated areas. The replacement of traditional vertical organizations for network structures allows firms to increase their degree of specialization, a development that is propelled by the increased international competition. It has forced firms to adopt the most efficient ways of organizing production, and to implement technologies that minimize slacks and enable firms to fulfil the requirements of individual customers. Cooperation through networks, which aims at integrating complementary competencies and intensifying transmission of knowledge between networks participants, is hence one strategy that firms have adopted to meet the challenges of a changing environment. An important factor in this evolution is, of course, the rapid advance in IT and the improved possibilities it brings with it to monitor and coordinate geographically dispersed activities. That implies a reduction in transaction cost, which allows firms to outsource activities that formerly were undertaken within the firms. Orders for goods and services can be transmitted through the Internet, and on-line information makes it easier for suppliers and customers to plan production to avoid bottlenecks and minimize storage costs.

That brings us to the second major trend in industrial organization—internationalization—where the deregulation of barriers to trade and capital that flows between different markets, coupled with expanding trade, has led to unprecedented global levels of foreign direct investments during the 1980s. Hence, firms began to take locational issues more seriously. Although foreign investments would seem primarily to affect large firms, it would, of course, also indirectly affect SMEs. First, a shift in location may imply changed supplier links, comprising elements of internationalization as well as levying new demands on former suppliers. Second, it means that SMEs operating on previously sheltered markets will to a larger extent be exposed to international competition. Similarly, the price-setting power of formerly protected firms will be reduced. In fact, the quest for change will be particularly obvious for the SMEs because large firms often have superior experience operating in an international environment characterized by fierce competition.

This gives rise to a number of questions associated with the so-called "new economy". Do small firms possess the specific knowledge required to meet such changed prerequisites in industrial production? Can knowledge variables be shown to have a positive effect on firm performance in terms of profitability and international competitiveness? What are the particular advantages of clusters and what drives their dynamics? How important is the interaction between the service sector—particularly venture capital firms—and manufacturing firms? Is the location of large firms determined by the prevalence of an existing stock of SMEs, indicating that a support structure of suppliers and adequate labor skills is present? Are such existing clusters, or support systems, more important in knowledge-intensive industries? The answers have important policy implications, not least for growth, as has been pointed out in the endogenous growth literature. The possibilities for sustainable long-term growth and welfare hinge largely on the industrial dynamics and flexibility of countries, that is, the capacity of individuals and firms to engage in knowledge-enhancing and value-adding activities.

1.2 Industrial Organization and the Role of SMEs

By the late 19th century, the conclusion was drawn that SMEs would gradually become marginalized in economic operations. For a long time this prophecy seemed to materialize as scale gained importance up to the late 1960s (Sengenberg, Loveman and Piore, 1990). Around that time, however, an increase in the share of employment allotted to SMEs started to show up in most industrialized countries despite differences in initial conditions, culture and the institutional framework. Although skepticism concerning the importance of

SMEs has been expressed (Brown, Hamilton and Medoff, 1990; Davis, Haltiwanger and Schuh, 1996),[1] there seems to be little doubt that a shift took place in the late 1960s and the early 1970s (see for instance Carlsson, 1989; Acs and Audretsch, 1990; Acs, Audretsch and Feldman, 1994; Commission of the European Communities 1990, 1992, 1994; Gallagher and Robson, 1994).

Among the first studies in which the increased importance of SMEs was recognized was Birch's analysis of job creation that originates in smaller firms. He purported that the overwhelming majority of new jobs were supplied by new and small firms. Birch's findings have been criticized. Sengenberger, Loveman and Piore (1990), for instance, claimed that Birch confused firms with establishments and that a large number of the new jobs attributed to small firms indeed resulted from the reorganization and downsizing of large firms. Yet, later studies, for example, the OECD reports of 1985 and 1992, as well as recent Swedish analyses (Davidsson, Lindmark and Olofsson, 1994, 1996), reached the same conclusion as that of Birch in the original study.

Industrial dynamics and innovations is another field where SMEs have lately experienced a reassessment (Kamien and Schwartz, 1975; Rothwell and Zegweld, 1982; Doctor, van der Haorst and Stokman, 1989; Carlsson and Braunerhjelm, 1994; Davidsson, Olofsson and Lindmark, 1994; Audretsch, 1995; Cohen and Klepper, 1996). Audretsch (1995) argues that even though the traditional knowledge production function, linking knowledge input (R&D) to innovative output, may be valid, it does not necessarily imply that large firms in isolation are the prime sources of such output. Doubtlessly they do undertake most knowledge production in terms of R&D, yet the environment in which firms operate may constitute the critical factor in separating failures from success. Consequently, spillovers from a large number of firms as well as from other agents (universities, research institutes, etc.) have a complementary effect on other firms' performance and R&D investments (Feldman, 1994; Saxenian, 1994). That may also explain the important innovative activities initiated by many small firms (Link and Rees, 1990).The transmission of knowledge is generally disregarded in macro-oriented models of growth, although it seems inevitable that small firms and individuals are crucial in this process (von Hippel, 1987; Carlsson and Braunerhjelm, 1994; Acs, Audretsch and Feldman, 1992; Acs, Audretsch and Feldman, 1994; Audretsch and Feldman, 1996). Consequently, the institutional setup that provides the rules of the game is decisive, not the least of which are the possibilities of collecting information, communicating and experimenting, when organizing knowledge-enhancing activities (North and Thomas, 1973; Rosenberg and Birdzell, 1986; Eliasson, 1991, 1996; Davis and Henrekson, 1996; Henrekson, 1996; Henrekson and Johansson, 1999).

The recognition of the mechanisms for transmitting knowledge is closely

---

[1] For a criticism of the work of Davis et al. (1993), see Davidsson (1995).

associated with the modifications in organizing industrial production that has emerged recently. In addition, the move towards a more decentralized and flatter organizations, at the same time that core competencies are emphasized, in many ways gives SMEs a new and extended role.[2] As the organization of industrial production has shifted toward networks and technological systems, linking firms electronically, an increased degree of specialization of the participants is made possible where economies of scale is gained on a higher level than that of the individual firm. For instance, several participants may in various ways contribute with knowledge inputs into each firm's production. This allows the operating scale of firms to remain relatively small. Hence, it is a Coasian argument where the lowering of transaction costs through the new technology has enabled a downsizing of firms (Coase, 1937).

1.3 Purpose, Methodology and Limitations

The purpose of this book is threefold. First, we investigate whether some of the elements in the so-called "new economy" can be supported empirically. In particular, we examine the importance of knowledge and size in firm performance measured as profitability and international competitiveness. The composition and determinants of the knowledge base of firms is considered, as are the explanations for the internationalization of firms, particularly the role of size. Is size important for exploiting economies of scale and for minimizing per-unit fixed costs in production structures characterized by networks?

Second, we analyze the driving forces of clusters by comparing the institutional setup of Sweden with that in a number of other countries. We also address the issue of the importance of high-tech clusters in attracting investments by large firms. Clusters, or agglomeration economies (also referred to as network externalities), are claimed to reduce production costs through externalities that originate in different kinds of spillovers.

The third objective is to explore the degree of internationalization and the knowledge base of Swedish firms in the manufacturing sector, distributed across different size classes. Part of this data set is implemented in the econometrics analyses in Chapters 3 and 4. In addition, we present the size distribution of firms for a large number of countries.

Although both theoretical and empirical issues are considered in the book, emphasis is on the empirical side. Hence, we scrutinize certain elements claimed to be the key ingredients of the "new economy". The analysis is strictly focused on microeconomic issues, whereas macro-oriented questions, such as the influence of the new economy on overall inflation, productivity, demand for

---

[2]See for instance Jarillo, 1988; Szarka, 1990; Markusen, 1996. For a Swedish perspective, see Johansson, Karlsson and Westin, 1994.

skills, and so forth, fall outside the scope of the book. Most of the data used in the empirical analyses have been collected through questionnaires and interviews. In some of the studies, these data are pooled with statistics from official sources. The exact procedures used for the collection of data and the methodology applied are explained in detail in the respective chapters.

The analysis is restricted to the manufacturing sector (with the exception of Chapter 5), which, of course, is a limitation because most SMEs can be found in the service sector. It is also in this sector that growth in numbers of firms and employees has been strongest in the last decades. Moreover, service companies have become important parts of the production networks that have evolved in recent years. Still, private services are closely tied to the production of goods. Furthermore, much of the empirical analysis is cross-sectional, implying that we cannot say much about the development over time.

1.4 Theoretical Background

A key issue that arises when discussing the theoretical background concerns the capability of SMEs to overcome the drawbacks of being small. Mill claimed by the mid-19th century that a tendency toward large-scale organization of businesses would lead to the demise of SMEs. This view was pursued—although for different reasons—by Marx and Schumpeter, and in the aftermath of the Industrial Revolution, the share of employment in large units did indeed increase. At present, however, rather the opposite finding prevails.[3]

What factors determine the size distribution of firms?[4] Even though the question may appear somewhat naive, several economists have been occupied by it over the years, particularly because economies of scale in production are a standard assumption in much of economic modeling. Scale economies seem, however, to become increasingly important for activities outside the actual production process. Examples of such activities are R&D, marketing, finance and so on, from which several production units within a firm can extract benefits. Hence, a distribution of a large number of small establishments may be compatible with a market dominated by large firms. Alternatively, firms may draw on benefits related to a cluster, for example, network economies of different kinds.

One reason for the changing size distribution of firms can be attributed to technological progress. On the one hand, production technology sets the limit

---

[3] The role of the entrepreneur, and the factors that are conducive for an entrepreneurial environment, are not addressed in this book. For an excellent overview, see Wennekers, Thurik and Buis (1997). See also Davidsson (1989).

[4] For a discussion of the size distribution, or convergence of size distribution, see also Gibrat (1931) and Jovanovic (1982). A survey of the literature can be found in Schmalensee (1989).

for the operating units. As technology improves over time, different vintages apply to different scales. Hence, the distribution of firm size has a time aspect. Furthermore, technological progress, paired with considerable reductions in the costs of acquiring new technology, has revolutionized SME flexibility (Carlsson, 1984; Johansson, 1991; Carlsson and Taymaz, 1992; Eliasson, 1996).[5] On the other hand, information technology also affects the plant size and the organization of production within the firm. It gives access to information at lower costs, and also makes information easier to process and interpret, which weakens the scale argument in production. However, it could also be argued that the establishment of larger firms is facilitated because the control and monitoring possibilities increase with improved information technology.

To explain the SME success, a number of sources of diseconomies of scale have been suggested that may offset potential economies of scale. These offsetting factors include, for example, limited supply of strategic factors, decreasing efficiency of factors as scale increases, disproportional increasing costs of management because of coordination and monitoring costs, decreasing motivation, and increasing selling and distribution costs. The scarcity of human capital and of entrepreneurial skill are especially regarded as constraints to growth (Lucas, 1978; Brock and Evans, 1986). Other deterrents to growth are small home country markets, difficulties in raising capital necessary for expansion and a higher degree of risk aversion (Aizenman and Marion, 1999; Ghoshal and Loungani, 1999). Access to capital has been viewed as a particularly severe restriction on firm growth, an issue which is also related to whether equity or loan financing can be obtained (Penrose, 1956; Horwitch and Pralahad, 1976; Buckley, 1986; Black and Gilson, 1998; Gompers, 1998; Lumme, Mason and Suomi, 1998).[6]

1.5 Internationalization

To start with, the meaning of internationalization has to be defined. In its general sense, it alludes to a wide range of international penetration and commitment, comprising exports, sales agents, and wholly owned production units abroad. Internationalization by SMEs predominantly takes the form of exports, whereas the setting up of subsidiaries abroad is less common.

---

[5] See also Sabel (1983) and Piore and Sabel (1984).

[6] Financial constraint is habitually regarded as a severe bottleneck for SMEs. Some studies, however, point in another direction. Lindquist (1991) for instance, in her study on small Swedish high-tech firms, finds little support for financial constraints, and similar results are reported for English SMEs (Burns and Dewhurst, 1986). The ongoing integration of financial markets also favors SMEs. However, during the transition from regulated to integrated markets, it is possible for financial institutions to charge SMEs higher costs by exploiting information differences (Oxelheim 1996).

Furthermore, export performance by SMEs differs widely between countries. The explanation is related to the different sizes of home country markets, the structure of the industry, governmental policies, and so forth.

A theoretical rationale for internationalization has been provided by Hymer (1960), Buckley and Casson (1992), Williamson (1975, 1985), Caves (1996) and others. In short, the argument is that the lack of markets for firm-specific assets (FSAs), or knowledge, induces firms to internalize production in wholly owned subsidiaries abroad. Arm's-length contracts are not possible because they may erode the firm-specific advantage through different kinds of opportunistic behavior. Therefore, firms prefer to expand through foreign direct investment (FDI) rather than through cooperative arrangements such as licensing. In fact, this argument can be attributed to Coase's explanation of the rationale of the firm (Coase, 1937). However, FSAs are not just given to firms; rather, they are acquired through R&D investments, which in most cases—though not always—require scale in production.[7]

A particular branch of the preceding theory is the behavioristic approach to explain internationalization, which is often regarded as particularly relevant for SMEs (Aharoni, 1966; Johansson and Vahlne, 1977). A sequential process is visualized where close markets—geographically and culturally—are first exploited. Expansion to other markets then gradually proceeds, both for markets and for means of internationalization; that is, export agents are substituted for sales affiliates, and, finally, producing subsidiaries are established.

A more novel framework is introduced by Porter (1980, 1990). He conceptualizes factors that generate specific skills and abilities in the so-called "diamond", which explicitly enumerate six factors that determine the competitiveness of firms from different nations. Since "diamonds" differ between countries, trade and internationalization takes place. Hence, the model has a factor-endowment flavor, although Porter stresses that favorable production conditions are partly created by firms themselves. He regards the ability to create such favorable conditions, which stems from the characteristics of the diamond, as the main determinant in sustaining competitiveness at the firm level. The interlinks to the industrial network approach are close, where emphasis is on the establishing and developing of networks in the internationalization process (Arthur, Hendry and Jones, 1991; Johanson and Mattson, 1984; Malecki, 1985; Markusen, 1996).

Turning to one of the main questions raised in this book, that is, the relation between knowledge capital, internationalization and size, let us consider the first attempt to combine these factors into an analytical framework, in which an eclectic approach was applied (Dunning, 1977). The OLI theory, rather than being a full theory, is a discussion of the conditions necessary for foreign

---

[7] Outsourcing of R&D has become a increasingly common way of organizing industrial knowledge upgrading, as evident from, for instance, so-called drug discovery companies.

production to take place. The OLI theory is named after the three main factors that influence FDI. Ownership advantages, that is, firm-specific assets, are represented by O, L stands for locational advantages in host countries, and I refers to the internalization of firms' proprietary assets. The lack of markets for firm-specific assets tends to make transaction costs—or the risk of being exposed to "opportunistic behavior" (Williamson, 1975)—excessively high for arm's-length contracts and similar arrangements, which induce internalization of production through FDI. For locational factors, the OLI theory maintains that, to attract FDI, the recipient country has to offer a particular, country-specific advantage. Such advantages include, for instance, sizable markets, access to specific skills, cost of production factors, or policy-designed incentives. These are necessary conditions for FDI; however, they are not sufficient because firms always have the option to substitute FDI for exports from the home country.

A more recent vein in this field of economic theory is the "new" locational literature, which focuses on the spatial distribution of production and the choice made by firms about the mode of internationalization (Markusen, 1995; Brainard, 1997; Braunerhjelm and Ekholm, 1998). Depending on the type of economies of scale and the level of trade costs, firms will either export from their home countries or set up a foreign plant in other countries. One aspect to which increased attention has been paid concerns agglomeration and cluster patterns, that is, why firms in a specific industry tend to be concentrated in certain geographically well-defined areas, even though costs are higher. The rationale for such agglomeration behavior is traditionally ascribed to the advantages arising from demand and supply linkages or intra-industry technological and information spillovers. In the former case, the possibility of being linked to networks of suppliers and distributions constitutes one reason for concentrate production (Krugman, 1991a, b; Venables 1996).

The size of the firm plays a key role in the choice of internationalization mode. Economies of scale are assumed to appear either at the firm or at the plant level; alternatively, they may be a mixture of the two. The first type of economies of scale is defined as emanating from knowledge-producing activities, for instance, R&D operations. Such knowledge can be used as a non-rivalry, blueprint asset in many plants, irrespective of their locations. Economies of scale that arise at the plant level must, however, be exploited at one particular location and require that a certain level of production can be attained at that specific location. Together with trade costs, the level and type of scale economies determine the mode of internationalization. Generally, high transportation costs induce FDI, even though economies of scale on the plant level may be high, whereas zero transportation costs tend to make all firms exporters.[8] Hence, size (scale) enters

---

[8] Another reason for agglomeration can be derived from the new-growth theory (Romer, 1986; Sala-i-Martin, 1990; Martin and Ottaviano, 1996). It is argued that knowledge-enhancing activities can only partly be appropriated by firms, implying that an externality is created and diffused to

as a decisive variable in determining the type and extent of internationalization.

The following general pattern can be derived from these locational models on the basis of the general equilibrium paradigm: whether firms penetrate foreign markets through exports or direct investments, they need to possess some kind of firm-specific assets. Furthermore, the choice between exports and foreign direct investments is partly dictated by the type of economies of scale. More particularly, the larger the economies of scale on the plant level, the larger the probability that the firm will pursue an export strategy. The costs of trade will also affect the chosen strategy; however, in the following chapters we focus on countries where Sweden has had more or less free trade for a long time, and hence we can disregard the trade-cost factor.

In summary, the theories that have been outlined all stress the importance of developing a firm-specific asset or unique product that leads to competitive capabilities that can be exploited abroad. Different-sized firms are associated with specific advantages as well as with disadvantages. Therefore, firms of different sizes are likely to cooperate and coexist, fulfilling different and complementary tasks, a conclusion advanced already by Marshall (1890). One indication of such coexistence is that, on average, profit levels of SMEs match large firms well and even surpass them in some cases (Aiginger and Tichy, 1984; Burns and Dewhurst, 1986; Braunerhjelm, 1991a, b).[9]

1.6 Organization of the Book

Even though the different chapters of the book are linked to each other in a coherent way, they are also self-contained and can thus be read separately from each other. The following Chapter 2 provides a detailed description of the size distribution of Swedish firms and contrasts this picture with the distribution in other countries. In addition, small, medium-sized and large firms are compared for factors judged as being critical to their ability to meet stronger competition in the future. Their internationalization and knowledge stocks are emphasized. Parts of these data are implemented in the empirical analyses in the following chapters.

In Chapters 3 and 4, the role of knowledge and size in explaining firm performance, that is, profitability and international competitiveness, is investigated. The determinants of knowledge assets are also examined, albeit from a different perspective and by implementing different methods. A

---

other firms, thereby reducing their costs (Griliches, 1979). In addition, firms may be induced for strategic reasons to set up foreign affiliates instead of to export.

[9] One explanation for the impressive profit performance by SMEs relates to different managerial organizations in SMEs and large enterprises. SMEs are claimed to be managed by owners who are more inclined to maximize profits than are hired management.

knowledge-stock variable is introduced that more closely relates to the theoretical concept of firm-specific assets. In addition to traditional R&D investments, this variable also takes into account the accumulation of assets in marketing, education and software. The analysis generates the following main results. First, we show the relationship of the firms' endowment of knowledge to the skill structure of their employees and the size of the firm. Interestingly enough, the impact of size on firms' endowments of knowledge is diminishing. This result can be interpreted as though, beyond a certain threshold, a further increase in size adds little to the knowledge endowment within the firm, indicating that the firm cannot efficiently handle too large an endowment of knowledge. Second, we find that large knowledge stock acts as a shift factor for firm profitability, whereas the influence of size, or market power, is negligible. Furthermore, size, together with firms' knowledge stocks, constitutes the main explanation for the degree of internationalization. Finally, different modes of internationalization seem to substitute for each other.

Chapters 5 and 6 explore issues related to agglomeration, clusters and networks. In Chapter 5, the role of institutions, venture capital and industrial dynamics is investigated. It is shown how critical the institutional setup is for promoting a dynamic business environment. Further, the role of venture capital firms and business angels as a bridge between ideas of entrepreneurs and the commercialization phase is emphasized. The analysis is based on detailed data of the Swedish venture capital market, which is compared with venture capital markets in other countries. In Sweden, the government sector has acted as the main "venture" capitalist, with meager results.

In Chapter 6, unique data on Swedish multinationals are combined with industry data for 18 countries, and the influence of host-country characteristics on the location of foreign production is analyzed. Particular attention is directed toward agglomeration tendencies in the firms' location. In most countries, the majority of firms are small; therefore, we argue that the prevalence of a large production sector can be used as a proxy for a large number of SMEs in that industry. If Swedish firms predominantly invest in countries that already have an abundance of similar production sectors, our interpretation is that the existence of a relatively large number of SMEs constitutes an attractive factor because large firms determine where to locate production. The results suggest that agglomeration effects are present, predominantly in technologically advanced industries. We also verify that market size, the supply of skilled labor and earlier export patterns affect the location of overseas production.

In Chapter 7, we conclude with a summary of the main findings. We also discuss to what extent the "new economy" exists and what is new about it. The policy implications are discussed, as are the avenues for future research in this area.

LITERATURE

Acs, Z. and D. Audretsch, 1990, *Innovation and Small Firms*, Cambridge: MIT Press.

Acs, Z., D. Audretsch and M. Feldman, 1992, Real Effects of Academic Research, *American Economic Review*, 82, 363-367.

Acs, Z., D. Audretsch and M. Feldman, 1994, R&D Spillovers and Recipient Firm Size, *Review of Economics and Statistics*, 100, 336-340.

Aharoni, Y., 1966, *The Foreign Investment Decision Process*, Cambridge, MA: Division of Research, Graduate School of Business Research, Harvard University.

Aiginger, K. and G. Tichy, 1984, Die Grösse die Kleine, *mimeo*, University of Graz, Austria.

Aizenman, J. and N. Marion, 1999, Volatility and Investment; Interpreting Evidence from Developing Countries, *Economica*, 67, forthcoming.

Arthur, M., C. Hendry and A. Jones, 1991, Learning From Doing: Adaptation & Resource Management in the Smaller Firms, *mimeo*, Presented at the 11th Annual Strategic Management Society International Conference, University of Warwick, England.

Audretsch, D., 1995, *Innovation and Industry Evolution*, Cambridge (MA.) and London: MIT Press.

Audretsch, D. and Z. Acs, 1991, Innovation and Size at the Firm Level, *Southern Economic Journal*, 57, 739-744.

Audretsch, D. and M. Feldman, 1996, Knowledge Spillovers and the Geography of Innovation and Production, *American Economic Review*, 86, 630-640.

Black, B. and Gilson, R., 1998, "Venture Capital and the Structure of Capital Markets: Bank Versus Stock Markets", *Journal of Financial Economics*, 47, 243-277.

Brainard, S., 1997, An Empirical Assessment of the Proximity-Concentration Tradeoff Between Multinational Sales and Trade, *American Economic Review*, 87, 520-544.

Braunerhjelm, P., 1991a, Svenska underleverantörer och småföretag - Struktur, internationalisering och kompetens, (Swedish Subcontractors and SMEs - Specialization, Internationalization and Competence), *Research Report 38*, Stockholm: The Research Institute of Industrial Economics (IUI).

Braunerhjelm, P., 1991b, Svenska underleverantörer och småföretag i det nya Europa, (Swedish Subcontractors and SMEs in the New Europe), *The Journal of the Economic Society of Finland*, 219-228.

Braunerhjelm, P. and K. Ekholm, 1998, *The Geography of Multinational Firms*, Boston, Dordrecht and London; Kluwer Academic Publishers.

Brock, W. and D. Evans, 1986, *The Economics of Small Business*, New York: Holmes&Meier.

Brown, C., J. Hamilton and J. Medoff, 1990, *Employers Large and Small*,

Cambridge, MA and London: Harvard University Press.

Buckley, P., 1986, Foreign Direct Investment by Small and Medium Sized Enterprises: The Theoretical Background, *mimeo*, Presented at the conference Project on Transfer of Technology to Developing Countries by Small and Medium Sized Enterprises, Nurnberg, Germany.

Buckley, P. and M. Casson, 1992, Organizing for Innovation: The Multinational Enterprise in the Twenty-first Century, in Buckley, P. and M. Casson, (eds.), *Multinational Enterprises in the World Economy*, Aldershot and Brookfield: Edward Elgar Publishing Ltd.

Burns, P. and J. Dewhurst, 1986, *Small Business in Europe*, London: MacMillan.

Carlsson, B., 1984, The Development and the Use of Machine Tools in Historical Perspective, *Journal of Economic Behavior and Organization*, 5, 90-111.

Carlsson, B., 1989, The Evolution of Manufacturing Technology and Its Impact on Industrial Structure: An International Study, *Small Business Economics*, 1, 21-37.

Carlsson, B. and P. Braunerhjelm, 1994, *Teknologiska system och ekonomisk tillväxt (Technological Systems and Economic Growth)*, Bilaga 10 till Långtidsutredningen 1994 in SOU 1995:4, Stockholm: Allmänna förlaget.

Carlsson, B. and E. Taymaz, 1992, Flexible Technology and Industrial Structure in the US, *WP 92.08*, Case Western Reserve University.

Caves, R., 1996, *Multinational Enterprises and Economic Analysis*, New York: Cambridge University Press.

Coase, R., 1937, The Nature of the Firm, *Economica*, 13, 169-182.

Cohen, W. and S. Klepper, 1996, A Reprise of Size and R&D, *Economic Journal*, 106, 1-14.

Commission of the European Communities, 1990, *Enterprises in the European Community*, Luxembourg.

Commission of the European Communities, 1992, *Enterprises in the European Community*, Luxembourg.

Commission of the European Communities, 1994, *Enterprises in the European Community*, Luxembourg.

Davidsson, P., 1989, *Continued Entrepreneurship and Small Firm Growth*, Stockholm: EFI.

Davidsson, P., 1995, Small Firms: Has their Role as Job Creators Been Exaggerated?, in Dunlop, W. and B. Gibson (eds.), *Skills for Success in Small and Medium Enterprises*, Proceedings of the ICSB 40th World Conference. Newcastle, Australia: Institute of Industrial Economics at the University of Newcastle.

Davidsson, P., L. Lindmark and C. Olofsson, 1994, *Dynamiken i svenskt näringsliv*, Lund: Studentlitteratur.

Davidsson, P., L. Lindmark and C. Olofsson, 1996, *Näringslivsdynamik under*

1990-talet, Stockholm: NUTEK.

Davis, S., J. Haltiwanger and S. Schuh, 1996, *Job Creation and Destruction*, Cambridge, MA: MIT Press.

Davis, S. and M. Henrekson, 1996, Industrial Policy, Employer Size and Economic Performance in Sweden, in Freeman, R., B. Swedenborg and R. Topel, *The Welfare State in Transition*, Chicago: University Press of Chicago.

Doctor, J., R. van der Haorst and C. Stokman, 1989, Innovation Processes in Small- and Medium-sized Companies, *Entrepreneurship and Regional Development*, 1, 33-53.

Dunning, J., 1977, Trade, Location of Economic Activities and the MNE: A Search for an Eclectic Approach, in Hesselborn, P.-O., B. Ohlin and P.-M. Wijkman (eds.), *The International Allocation of Economic Activity*, London: MacMillan.

Eliasson, G., 1991, Modelling the Experimentally Organized Economy—Complex Dynamics in an Empirical Micro-Macro Model of Endogenous Growth, *Journal of Economic Behaviour and Organization*, 16, 153-182.

Eliasson, G., 1996, *Firm Objectives, Controls and Organization*, Boston, Dordrecht and London: Kluwers Academic Publisher.

EVCA & KPMG, 1998, *European Venture Capital Association Yearbook 1998*, Zaventum (www.evca.com) and London.

Feldman, M., 1994, *The Geography of Innovation*, Boston: Kluwer Academic Publishers.

Gallagher, C. and B. Robson, 1994, Change in the Size Distribution of UK Firms, *Small Business Economics*, 6, 299-312.

Gibrat, R., 1931, *Les Inégalités Économiques. Applications: Aux Inégalités des Richesses, a la Concentration des Enterprises, Aux Populations des Villes, Aux Statistiques des Familles, etc., d'une Loi Nouvelle: La Loi de l'Effet Proportionell*, Paris: Librairie du recueil Sirey.

Ghoshal, V. and Loungani, P., 1999, The Differential Impact of Uncertainty on Investments in Small and Large Businesses, HWWA Diskussionspapier 81, Hamburg.

Gompers, P., 1996, "Grandstanding in the Venture Capital Industry", *Journal of Financial Economics*, 42, 133-156.

Griliches, Z., 1979, Issues in Assessing the Contribution of Research and Development to Productivity Growth, *The Bell Journal of Economics*, 10, 92-116.

Henrekson, M., 1996, *Företagandets villkor*, Stockholm: SNS Förlag.

Henrekson, M. and D. Johansson, 1999, Institutional Effects on the Evolution of the Size Distribution of Firms, *Small Business Economics*, 12, 11-23.

Horwitch, M., and C. Pralahad, 1976, Managing Technological Innovation—Three Ideal Modes, *Sloan Management Review*, 17, 77-89.

von Hippel, E., 1987, *The Source of Innovation*, Oxford University Press, New

York.
Hymer, S., 1960, *The International Operations of National Firms: A Study of Direct Foreign Investments*, MIT Press, Cambridge, MA.
Jarillo, J., 1988, On Strategic Networks, *Strategic Management Journal*, 9, 31-41.
Johansson, B., 1991, Regional Industrial Analysis and Vintage Dynamics, *Regional Science*, 25, pp. 1-18.
Johansson, B., C. Karlsson and L. Westin, 1994, *Patterns in a Network Economy*, Berlin, London and New York: Springer-Verlag.
Johanson, J. and L.-G. Mattson, 1984, Internationalization in Industrial Systems—A Network Approach, Presented at the conference Prince Bertils Symposium on Strategies in Global Competition, Stockholm School of Economics, Stockholm, Sweden.
Johansson, J. and J.-E. Vahlne, 1977, The Internationalization Process of the Firm—A Model of Knowledge Development and Increasing Foreign Market Commitments, *Journal of International Business Studies*, 8, 23-32.
Jovanovic, B., 1982, Selection and Evolution of Industry, *Econometrica*, 50, 649-670.
Kamien, M. and N. Schwartz, 1975, Market Structure and Innovation: A Survey, *Journal of Economic Literature*, 13, 1-37.
Krugman, P., 1991a, Increasing Returns and Economic Geography, *Journal of Political Economy*, 99, 483-500.
Krugman, P., 1991b, *Geography and Trade*, MIT Press, Cambridge, MA.
Lerner, J., 1998, "Angel Financing and Public Policy: An Overview", *Journal of Banking and Finance*, 22, 773-783.
Lindquist, M., 1991, *Infant Multinationals: The Internationalization of Young, Technology-Based Swedish Firms*, Stockholm: IIB.
Link, A. and J. Rees, 1990, Firm Size, University Based Research, and the Returns to R&D, *Small Business Economics*, 2, 25-32.
Lucas, R., 1978, On the Size Distribution of Business Firms, *Bell Journal of Economics*, 9, 508-523.
Lumme, A., Mason, C. and Suomi, M., 1998, *Informal Venture Capital*, Kluwer Academic Publishers, Boston, Dordrect, and London.
Malecki, E., 1985, Industrial Location and Corporate Organization in High-Technology Industries, *Economic Geography*, 61, 345-369.
Markusen, J., 1995, Incorporating the Multinational Enterprise into the Theory of International Trade, *Journal of Economic Perspectives*, 9, 169-189.
Markusen, A., 1996, Sticky Place in Slippery Space: A Topology of Industrial Districts, *Economic Geography*, 72, 293-331.
Marshall, A.,1890, *Principles of Economics*, London, England.
Martin, P. and G. Ottaviano, 1996, Growing Locations: Industry Location in a Model of Endogenous Growth, *CEPR Discussion Paper*, No. 1523.
North, D. C. and Thomas, R.P., 1973, *The Rise of the Western World: A New*

Economic History. Cambridge: Cambridge University Press.

OECD, 1992, *OECD Employment Outloo*k, OECD, Paris.

OECD, 1995, *OECD Employment Outlook*, OECD, Paris.

Oxelheim, L., 1996, *Financial Markets in Transition. Globalization. Investment and Economic Growth*, London: Routledge.

Penrose, E., 1956, Foreign Investment and Growth of the Firm, *Economic Journal*, 66, 220-235.

Piore, M. and C. Sabel, 1984, *The Second Industrial Divide: Possibilities for Prosperity*, New York: Basic Books.

Porter, M., 1980, *Competitive Strategy*, New York: Free Press.

Porter, M., 1990, *The Competitive Advantage of Nations*, London and Basingstoke: MacMillan.

Romer, P., 1986, Increasing Returns and Economic Growth, *American Economic Review*, 94, 1002-1037.

Rosenberg, N. and Birdzell, L. E., 1986, *How the West Grew Rich: The Economic Transformation of the Industrial World*. London: Tauris.

Rothwell, R. and W. Zegweld, 1982, *Innovation and the Small and Medium Sized Firm—Their Role in Employment and in Economic Change*, London: Francis Pinter.

Sabel, C., 1983, Italian Small Business Development: Lessons for US Industrial Policy, in Zysman, J. and L. Tyson (eds.), *American Industry in International Competition*, New York: Cornell University Press.

Sala-i-Martin, X., 1990, Lecture Notes on Economic Growth, *WP 3563 and 3564*, NBER, Cambridge.

Saxenian, A.,1994, *Regional Networks: Industrial Adaptation in Silicon Valley and Route 128*, Cambridge, MA: Harvard University Press.

Schmalensee, R., 1989, Inter-Industry Studies of Structure and Performance, in Schmalensee, R. and R. Willig (eds.), *Handbook of Industrial Organization*, Oxford: North Holland.

Sengenberger, W., G. Loveman and M. Piore, 1990, *The Re-emergence of Small Enterprises: Industrial Countries*, Geneva: ILO.

Szarka, J., 1990, Networking and Small Firms, *International Small Business Journal*, 8, 10-22.

Venables, A., 1996, Equilibrium Locations of Vertically Linked Industries, *International Economic Review*, 37, 341-359.

Wennekers, S., R. Thurik and F. Buis, 1997, *Entrepreneurship, Economic Growth and What Links Them Together*, Zoetermeer: EIM.

Williamson, O., 1975, *Market and Hierarchies: Analysis and Antitrust Implications*, New York: Free Press.

Williamson, O., 1985, *The Economic Institutions of Capitalism*, New York: Free Press.

Chapter 2

THE SIZE DISTRIBUTION OF FIRMS: SOME STYLIZED FACTS

2.1 Introduction

A significant characteristic of industrial organization in the postwar era, at least up to the 1980s, is the establishment of large international firms, designed for mass-production of standardized goods. For a number of reasons, traditional wisdom has regarded production by smaller units as inferior, where small firms eventually were expected to more or less wither away. However, since the beginning of the 1970s the increasing role of small and medium sized enterprises (SMEs) in terms of employment and value-added has prompted a revaluation of the importance of SMEs.[10] In this chapter we will provide an international comparison of the size distribution of firms in Sweden and in other industrialized countries. We will briefly review how the size distribution has emerged in different countries and discuss the main causes behind this development (sections 2.2 and 2.3). Moreover, we will also present a detailed comparison of the differences between small firms, medium-sized firms and large firms in order to asses the structural factors forming the capabilities and competitiveness of firms of different size classes (section 2.4).

This section will largely be based on data on Swedish firms. In the proceeding chapters we will then empirically investigate some of the factors that seem crucial for international competitiveness, such as the skill composition of the labor force, the importance of economies of scale, and the sources of scale effects. The chapter is concluded by a discussion on the prospects for small scale production (section 2.5).

2.2 The Shift Toward SME-Production in Industrialized Countries

Ever since Birch's (1979, 1981) studies on SMEs—which indicated that approximately 80 percent of employment growth emanated from SMEs—attention has been directed towards employment effects of SMEs. A

---

[10] See Sengenberger, Loveman and Piore (1990), arguing that this trend started already in the end of the 1960s for most of the industrialized world. See also Burns and Dewhurst (1986) and OECD Employment Outlook (1985). Cantwell and Radaccio (1990) shows that on average the size of multinational firms has decreased. Carlsson (1989) showed that the role of the Fortune 500 firms in the US diminished in the 1980s. Also, Carlsson (1992) and Johansson (1997) analyzes the causes of the shift towards small business internationally and explores the consequences for industrial structure and competitiveness.

comparative study of the development of SMEs in the industrialized world— in terms of primarily employment shares—was first systematically analyzed by Burns and Dewhurst (1986) and Sengenberger, Loveman and Piore (1990). These studies both report an increase in the share of employment, despite bottlenecks in financial resource, managerial know-how, etc. In Sengenberg et al (1990), the authors set off with the following statement. "Just a decade ago the idea that small enterprises might be seen as the key to economic regeneration, and a road to renewed growth of employment and the fight against mass unemployment, may have seemed eccentric or even absurd. Today this view seems much less far fetched. On the contrary, many observers from different traditions and political orientations embrace the idea, though they may disagree on why and how small firm expansion and dynamism have arisen". A decade later this quote is still valid.

In all the countries covered in the studies mentioned above, an apparent shift towards smaller units of production in terms of employment in the postwar period is reported.[11] Moreover, in all countries—with one exception—this development coincides with a loss of the large firm's part of manufacturing employment. It is also remarkable how robust these findings are despite the differences between countries with regard to industrial structure, institutional setting, size distribution, different legal framework, tradition and history. However, although the trend is similar in various countries, the extent of SME growth differs quite substantially among the countries.[12]

In Tables 2.1 and 2.2 it is shown how the employment share of small enterprises and establishments have evolved during the last three to four decades. Most countries seem to have experienced a shift towards an increasing share of employment in smaller units in the late 1960s or in the beginning of the 1970s. This is particularly evident for establishment data on the total economy where a quite clear U-shaped pattern of small firms employment share emerges (Table 2.2).

As mentioned above, SMEs are most important in the service sector and the size distribution in the total economy may therefore be influenced by the expanding service sector. However, this shift in composition explains only part of the drift towards smaller production units (Sengenberg et al, 1990). As shown in Table 2.3-2.4, even if the manufacturing sector is isolated, the tendency towards smaller units remains (with the exception of Switzerland), even though it is weaker. If establishment size is studied, the pattern is more clear-cut (Tables

---

[11] The countries are Denmark, France, Italy, Japan, Northern Ireland, Switzerland, The Republic of Ireland, The United Kingdom, The United States and West Germany. The same pattern is observed in Canada (Laroche, 1989).

[12] Data on establishments are often more reliable then firm data. In Sengenberger's et al study, data have sometimes been collected from different sources which may influence the time series. In Tables 2.1-2.4, small implies less than 100 employees while medium refers to less than 500 employees, if nothing else is stated.

2.2 and 2.4).

A picture of a movement towards decentralized organization structures emerges since both enterprise and establishment sizes are diminished. Furthermore, the authors argue that size in itself is not decisive for performance but rather the organization of production and the underlying structure in terms of policies, networks etc. There is no evidence that sectoral small or cyclical factors determine the expansion of SMEs. Instead, the expansion of SMEs seems to be connected with increased heterogeneity in consumer demand and the implementation of new technology allowing flexibility and high quality production.

Table 2.1. Employment shares by enterprise size, time series for the total economy.

Japan	1965	1968	1971	1974	1977	1982	1985
Small	53.7	55	55.9	57	58.9	60	73
Medium*			70	70.4	72.7	73.1	
United States	1958	1963	1967	1972	1977	1982	
Small	41.3	39.9	39.9	41.3	40.1	45.7	
Medium	55.1	52.9	53.2	53.5	52.5	58.7	
France			1971		1979		1985
Small			39		43.4		46.2
Medium			57.4		60.7		64.5
West Germany	1961		1970				
Small**	54.9		52.3				
Italy	1951	1961	1971			1981	
Small	60.2	63.5	61.6			69.3	
Medium	73	77.1	74.4			81.5	
Switzerland	1955	1965		1975			1985
Small***	52.5	45.4		46.1			46.3
Medium	82	78.9		77.4			73.4

Note: * 1-300 employees ** 1-200 employees *** 1-50 employees.
Source: Sengenberger et al (1990).

Table 2.2. Employment shares by establishment size, time series for the total economy.

Japan		1969	1972	1975	1978	1981	
Small		70.1	71.5	73.8	76.1	77.1	
Medium*		83.1	84.2	85.6	87.5	88.3	
United States	1962	1965	1970	1975	1978	1982	1985
Small	51.3	51.5	49.5	54	54.4	55.1	55.9
Medium				76.9	77.7	78.6	79.8
West Germany			1977	1979	1981	1983	1985
Small			47	47.9	48.3	49.7	49.6
Medium			70.4	71.1	71.4	72.3	72.3
Italy	1951	1961	1971			1981	
Small	67.2	61.6	69			72.4	
Medium	82.6	82.2				87.3	
Switzerland				1975			1985
Small				66.2			69.3
Medium				88.2			89

Note: * 1-300 employees.
Source: Sengenberger et al (1990).

Table 2.3. Employment shares by enterprise size, time series for the manufacturing sector.

Japan*	1955		1972	1975	1979	1983	
Small	57		43	45	49	47	
Medium	85		63	65	68	67	
United States	1958	1963	1967	1972	1977	1982	
Small	20.6	19.1	16.3	16.2	16.2	17.6	
Medium	37.1	34.5	30.4	28.9	29	30.3	
France			1971		1979		
Small			26.4		28.6		
Medium			49.5		50.6		
W. Germany**	1963		1970	1976	1980	1983	1984
Small	14		12.5	13.1	15.4	16	16.2
Medium	39.6		37.3	38	40.4	40.8	41.1
Italy**	1951	1961	1971			1981	
Small	50.5	53.2	50.5			55.3	
Medium	67.4	72	69.2			73.9	
Switzerland		1965					1985
Small		34.8					29.7
Medium		71					69.4
U. Kingdom			1971	1975	1978	1981	
Small			15.5	16.8	17.3	20.3	

Note: * In 1955 small is defined as 5-99 employees and medium size as 5-999 employees. **
Handicraft is included in the figures for 1980, 1983 and 1985. *** Small is defined as 1-49
employees.
Source: Sengenberger et al (1990).

Table 2.4. Employment shares by establishment size, time series for the manufacturing sector.

Japan	1957	1962	1971	1977	1980	1982	1984
Small	59	52	51	56	58	56	55
Medium*	73	68	67	71	74	72	72
United States			1974	1978	1980	1982	1985
Small			24.4	25.3	25.2	26.9	27.6
Medium			57.2	58.3	58.2	59.6	61.4
France	1954	1966		1974		1981	
Small	52	48		45		47	
Medium	75	74		72		73	
West Germany**	1963		1970	1976	1980		1984
Small	20		18.5	19.6	18.3		18.6
Medium	48		46.6	48.3	47.6		48.5
Italy	1951	1961	1971			1981	
Small	54.2	56.9	54.6			59.1	
Medium	74.6	78.5	76.9			80.3	
Switzerland	1955	1965			1975		1985
Small	43.6	37.8			38.4		33.3
Medium	80.1	76.8			78.3		77
United Kingdom	1954	1963	1970	1975			1983
Small	24.2	20.2	18.4	19.7			26.2
Medium	56.5	50.9	45.4	45			53.2
Sweden		1968	1973	1978	1983		1988
Small		39	35.3	27.5	28.2		23.7
Medium		52.7	48.9	40.8	41.7		37.9

Note: * Medium is defined as 100-299 employees. ** After 1976 the figures include handicraft sector.
Source: Sengenberger et al (1990) and own calculations.

Burns and Dewhurst (1986), and later the European Commission, report similar results where all countries except one belong to the Community. Irrespective of whether countries are small or large a pattern of growing SME sectors is quite evident. Their result contrasts with the general assumption that harmonization within the EC has primarily benefited large firms. Moreover, the process of concentration observed in the 1950s and 1960s has, according to the authors, not only ceased, but also been reversed.

2.3 Evidence after 1980 on the Size Distribution of Firms in Industrialized Countries

The following section gives a brief overview of the size distribution of firms in a number of European countries, with special emphasis on Sweden[13]. The classification of firms on different sizes is based on the official general industrial classification system used by Eurostat (Commission of European Communities, 1992), which differ from the more crude definition previously used. We will adopt the following size classification: small (10-99 employees), medium (100-499), and large firms (>500 employees). In the presentation of the Swedish statistics, up to nine different size classes will be used, covering the time period (1968-1993). In the comparison of the size distribution of firms in 12 European countries a somewhat less extensive time period will be considered (1983-1991)

Commencing with 12 European countries, Table 2.5 gives the number and ranking of small firms per inhabitants for all sectors, while Table 2.6 report the corresponding figures for the industrial sector (comprising extraction, manufacturing and energy.).

With regard to Table 2.5, the largest relative number of small firms is found in Luxembourg, Denmark and Germany. If only the industrial sector is considered, then Italy, Portugal and Denmark have the largest population of small firms. In both tables Sweden is ranked as having a comparatively limited number of small firms.

Looking at the overall distribution of firms, Sweden gains a top position in terms of large firms (Table 2.7). That holds for the total population as well as for industrial firms. Sweden is followed by Finland, France, Germany and United Kingdom when the total population is considered, and Belgium, Finland and the United Kingdom when it comes to industrial firms. Hence, the size distribution of firms differs quite dramatically between countries. Judging from the overall picture, it is obvious that the Swedish distribution of firms is skewed toward large firms.

---

[13] This section relies heavily on Johansson (1997), who gives a detailed description of the size distribution of firms within the European countries and the pitfalls associated with statistics of SMEs.

Table 2.5. The number of small-sized (10 - 99 employees) enterprises/1,000,000 inhabitants, all sectors, 1983-1991.

Country	1983	1986	1988	1989	1990	1991	Aver.	Rank
Germany	3946	3976	4070		3925		3979	3
France	2238	2151	2238		2412		2260	12
UK	3298	3365	2818	2841	3158	3084	3094	6
Sweden	2665	2800	2918	3012	3101	3074	2928	7
Italy	5179	5041	2235	2289			3686	4
Spain	2270	2278	2681	2984	2802	2828	2641	10
Belgium	2235	2226	2460	2582	2328	2408	2373	11
Portugal		2598			3257	3507	3121	5
Denmark			5220	5182	3005	2934	4085	2
Luxemb.	3329	3532	4286		4808	5207	4232	1
Finland			2830	2920	2896	2549	2799	9
Norway					2854		2854	8
Total	25159	27968	31757	21810	34546	25590		
Average	3145	3108	3176	3116	3141	3199	3147	

Note: In the last two observations for Italy, NACE 9, other services is excluded. The geographical coverage for Germany is the former Federal Republic of Germany. Belgium and Denmark have other reporting units than enterprise, e.g. establishments. The data for Belgium, Denmark, Spain, Italy and Luxembourg are produced using other sources of information in 1983 and 1986 than in the other years. Primary sectors are excluded. For Sweden, enterprises active in non-market services and public administration are included.
Source: Johansson (1997).

Table 2.6. The number of small-sized (10 - 99 employees) enterprises/1,000,000 inhabitants, industry (isic 2-4, 1983-1991).

Country	1983	1986	1988	1989	1990	1991	Aver.	Rank
Germany	1005	994	1203		1170		1093	4
France	670	646	649		689		663	10
UK	590	613	688	672	637	603	634	11
Sweden	750	775	782	784	785	746	770	8
Italy	1651	1374	1341	1390			1439	1
Spain	958	925	975	1042	1058	1145	1017	5
Belgium	713	703	663	687	678	684	688	9
Portugal		1084			1449	1559	1364	2
Denmark	1345	1516	1305	1295	971	955	1231	3
Luxemb.	495	546	638		669	698	609	12
Finland			803	832	800	711	787	7
Norway			977	933	775		895	6
Total	8177	9177	10024	7634	9681	7101		
Average	909	918	911	954	880	888	910	

Source: Johansson (1997).

Table 2.7. The size distribution of firms in 12 EU countries, percentage, 1991.

Country	All sectors			Industry		
	S	M	L	S	M	L
Germany	92.3 (5)	6.5 (8)	1.2 (6)	86.0 (7)	11.3 (6)	2.7 (6)
France	91.2 (7)	7.3 (6)	1.6 (5)	86.1 (6)	11.3 (5)	2.6 (7)
UK	89.7 (12)	8.7 (2)	1.6 (4)	84.8 (10)	11.9 (4)	3.3 (2)
Sweden	90.2 (10)	8.0 (3)	1.8 (1)	84.3 (11)	12.0 (3)	3.7 (1)
Italy	96.3 (1)	3.2 (12)	.5 (12)	94.5 (1)	4.8 (12)	.7 (12)
Spain	93.7 (2)	5.5 (11)	.8 (11)	92.2 (2)	6.8 (11)	.9 (11)
Belgium	90.7 (9)	7.6 (4)	1.7 (3)	85.0 (9)	12. 0 (2)	3.0 (5)
Portugal	92.3 (6)	6.8 (7)	.9 (10)	89.0 (4)	9.7 (9)	1.3 (10)
Denmark	93.4 (3)	5.7 (10)	1.0 (9)	88.7 (5)	9.8 (8)	1.5 (9)
Luxemb.	90.1 (11)	8.8 (1)	1.1 (7)	78.7 (12)	18.1 (1)	3.2 (3)
Finland	91.0 (8)	7.3 (5)	1.7 (2)	86.0 (8)	11.1 (7)	3.0 (4)
Norway	92.5 (4)	6.4 (9)	1.1 (8)	89.3 (3)	8.6 (10)	2.1 (8)

Note: S denotes small, M represents medium and L stands for large firms. Rank within parentheses.
Source: Johansson (1997).

Focussing at the size distribution of firms in Sweden, Table 2.8 reveals that for the overall population, the largest increases have occurred in the smallest and the largest size class over the period 1968-1993. Medium-sized firms has diminished over this period. This pattern is even stronger when the analysis is confined to the manufacturing sector. All size classes have experienced a decline during 1968-1993, except for the smallest class containing self-employed or one employee firms. The decline is strongest in the segments having 10 to 199 employees, while the decrease in the two largest size classes was about 50 percent lower (Table 2.9). This pattern of a decrease in predominantly the medium-sized firms is reinforced when the data set is corrected for state-owned enterprises and concerns (Johansson, 1997). It indicates a prevalence of factors that tend to deter growth of firms.

Table 2.8. The number of enterprises/1.000.000 inhabitants in Sweden, 1968-93.

Size class	1968	1993	Change 1968-1993 (%)
0-1	15474	39885	158
2-4	6232	7598	22
5-9	2587	3196	24
10-19	1404	1599	14
20-49	909	916	1
50-99	307	283	-8
100-199	152	141	-7
200-499	88	95	8
500+	57 (86)	92	61 (7)
Total	27210	53806	98

Note: From 1979 and on, county councils and municipalities are included in the statistics, which has a large effect on the number of large enterprises. The numbers in parentheses show the number of enterprises and the change thereof if 1979 is used as base year. Data concerning the smallest size class are uncertain due to statistical problems. Before 1986 the primary sector was excluded from the data, which explains the huge increase among the smallest firms (0-1).

Table 2.9. Enterprises/1,000,000 inhabitants 1968-1993, manufacturing.

Size class	1968	Min Value	Min Year	Max. Value	Max. Year	1993	Change 1968-1993 (%)
0-1	945	782	1976	4081	1986	2725	188.26
2-4	806	682	1982	847	1990	780	-3.21
5-9	547	472	1983	561	1970	479	-12.48
10-19	410	281	1993	430	1970	281	-31.32
20-49	318	222	1993	325	1973	222	-30.03
50-99	124	90	1993	138	1970	90	-27.21
100-199	72	49	1993	75	1969	49	-31.11
200-499	42	36	1993	43	1970	36	-15.49
500+	30	26	1993	36	1989	26	-14.53
Total	3294					4689	42.35

Source: Johansson (1997).

To summarize, Sweden turns out as being well endowed with large firms in an international comparison and ranks low with regard to the share of small firms. With regard to medium-sized firms, Sweden seems to be placed somewhere in the middle. On the other hand, looking more closely at Sweden's size distribution of firms over time, medium-sized firms have fared worse than other size classes. The most spectacular growth has occurred among the smallest firms. To get a clearer picture of the forces behind this growth, a more careful analysis of the motive behind entry must be considered.[14]

2.4 Internationalization, Knowledge and Specialization; Evidence from a Sample of Swedish Firms

In this section structural differences across large, medium-sized and small firms are described. To achieve this end a comparison is undertaken between Swedish large firms and SMEs with regard to primarily the level of knowledge and internationalization, and to some extent the firms' degree of specialization.

The data used in the present study were collected through a questionnaire sent directly to a sample of 230 SMEs manufacturing firms. Small firms are defined as firms employing between 20 and 200 persons, while medium-sized firms have less than 500 employees and large firms are consequently defined as those with an employment level exceeding 500.[15] Small and medium-sized firms will be referred to as SMEs. Some of the characteristics of the respective groups are revealed in Table 2.10.

2.4.1 Production Specialization of SMEs

In our sample, small firms are specialized in relatively more sophisticated goods than medium-sized firms, often adapted to their customers specific requirements. Less then 50 percent of their production can be classified into standard component production or simple processing of raw material. The picture is quite different for medium-sized firms. Approximately 75 percent of their production falls into the production categorized as simple, requiring

---

[14] One interpretation of the pattern is that new firms have stayed small, i.e. the increase in 0-1 size class means that these are only part-time firms, and that the main source of income stems from employment in some other occupation. At the same time some of the medium-sized firms has grown into the large size classes, which diminish their percentages shares, simultaneously as the small firms stay small, i.e. there is no adding to the medium-sized classes. In the period the turnover limits for firms to be included in the statistics has also changed (1987 and 1991). Similarly, full-time employee equivalents have been replaced by number of employees, irrespective of how much they work (1983).

[15] This database will also be implemented in some of the empirical studies to follow in the subsequent chapters.

relatively little input of technology and skill.[16]

Table 2.10. Average employment, turnover and rates of return for small and medium-sized firms, 1990.

	Employment (annual average)	Turnover (million SEK)	Rate of return on total capital (%)	Gross margin (%)
Small firms	53	30	n.a.	9
Medium-sized firms	220	100	9.9	7.3

Source: Braunerhjelm 1991a.

Another characteristic feature of medium-sized firms is that they have considerably closer links to large Swedish MNFs. In a process of intensified internationalization of customer firms, these firms encounter special requirements in their adaptation to the new conditions, partly due to that many of these firms are subcontractors to larger firms. They have to ponder whether they themselves should internationalize, i.e., follow their customers and set off a bandwagon effect, or seek alternative ways of serving their customers. An internationalization process is also associated with considerable financial risks and requires special competencies among the employees, a matter which will be somewhat elaborated further below. In contrast to medium-sized firms the group of small firms seems to be in a quite different position. The dependence on Swedish MNFs is much less pronounced, and the major part of customers belong to non-MNFs, sited in the local environment.

Looking at firms specialized in different types of production, it is evident that more sophisticated producers of systems and investment goods are less dependent on Swedish MNFs in the medium-size category. Notably, most of the exports can be found within the group which produce systems, suggesting that these firms have developed a certain skill— niche production— on which they base their international competitiveness. In the small firm category, exports are generally lower and the smallest systems producers are closely tied to the Swedish MNFs. Hence, one interpretation is that the smallest systems producers initially supply the large, advanced customers on the home market and, as they become bigger, turn to the international market. Such a development could be explained in terms of lack of knowledge of the foreign market, striving to reduce

---

[16] For a detailed description of the production categories, see Braunerhjelm (1991).

risks and costs by taking advantage of their customers' relations, etc.

2.4.2 The Knowledge Base of Small, Medium and Large Sized Firms

The database also contains information on the firms' knowledge base. Knowledge is a multi-dimensional concept and there is no generally accepted definition.[17] It includes competence in production, marketing, organization, distribution, R&D etc., that is, all the elements that constitute the ability to run a business successfully. It will always be tacit to a certain extent, partly related to entrepreneurial capacity, but also due to luck and other non-measurable factors. Despite the difficulties associated with the measurement of knowledge the 230 firms were asked to give information on a limited number of variables related to specific knowledge variables. These were R&D expenditures, marketing and education expenditures and finally, the composition of the labor force within firms.[18] In fact, for all of the knowledge variables a comparison will be made between large, medium-sized and small firms.[19]

In Table 2.11 the average expenditures on R&D, marketing and education—as reported in the firms' financial statements—are given. The difference between large firms and the SMEs is striking. R&D expenditures are six times higher in large firms than in medium-sized and about 11 times higher than in smaller firms. In marketing, although for the majority of large firms only domestic marketing expenditure is included, large firms display the highest expenditures, especially compared to medium-sized. This reflects the close links

Table 2.11. R&D, marketing, and education expenditures as percentage of total costs in small firms, medium-sized and large firms, 1990.

	R&D	Marketing	Education
Small firms	.8	4	.3
Medium-sized firms	1.5	3	2
Large firms (1989)	9	5	2

Source: Braunerhjelm, 1990, 1991a.

---

[17] For a discussion of business competence, its composition, and the evolution of the concept in the economic literature, see Carlsson and Eliasson (1991).

[18] The firms have also been asked to define a stock variable of their knowledge assets, which will be discussed in Chapters 3 and 4.

[19] Data on large firms emanates from a survey to 260 firms in 1989 (Braunerhjelm 1990).

that medium-sized firms have to a limited number of customers which makes marketing efforts less urgent. Education costs are more evenly dispersed between firms of different size, even though the SMEs report the smallest figures. On the other hand, as in-depth interviews with the firms reveal, less formal and more "on the job" training seems to be particularly important in the group of small firms.

Table 2.12 attempts to capture the knowledge base of firms from a somewhat different angle, that is, through the differences in the composition of the labor force in the three groups of firms. The five skill categories are ranked in descending order with regard to competence, defined as their profession status, not formal training and education. Notably, large firms have more than 40 percent of their labor force in the three higher skill categories whereas medium-sized firms are dominated by the least skilled employees.

Table 2.12. The skill composition of the labor force in small firms, medium-sized and large firms, 1990.

	Small	Medium-sized firms	Large firms (1989)
Executive staff	5	3	2
Specialists, middle management	9	7	11
White collar	16	15	29
Skilled worker	46	35	25
Unskilled worker	24	40	33
Total	100	100	100

Source: Braunerhjelm, 1990, 1991a.

The interpretation is that large firms, working in highly competitive international markets, are dependent on a large and sophisticated internal "service" sector, necessary to sustain and upgrade their international competitiveness. It is within these services activities that strategic competencies and competitiveness are created. Areas like marketing, finance, computer knowledge, logistics, and R&D, are of crucial importance.

These functions do not necessarily have to be produced within the firm, much can actually be produced from external suppliers. An increase towards external suppliers can also be observed throughout the 1990s, partly due to increased outsourcing and strategies geared towards core production. If these functions are necessary for international competitiveness, then the gap between large firms and particularly medium-sized firms is obvious. Note that the small firms are more abundantly endowed with skilled personnel than medium-sized.

2.4.3 Internationalization

In marked contrast to the ample studies on the internationalization of Swedish large firms (Swedenborg, 1979, 1986; Andersson et al, 1996; Braunerhjelm and Ekholm, 1998) less attention has been directed towards SMEs. Our final structural variable, the degree of internationalization, shows marked differences between firms of different size classes. Two variables are normally implemented to measure internationalization; export intensity and the extent of foreign production. As regard the latter variable—the extent of foreign production—it is well-known that large Swedish firms have since long had a substantial part of their operation located abroad. On average, Swedish multinationals firms had about 70 percent of their employees abroad (Braunerhjelm and Ekholm, 1998). For obvious reasons, foreign production by SMEs is modest, in 1990 it was estimated to account for between .5 an 1 percent of their production, and more than 95 percent of their employment is in their home country units. Still, over the last 30 years the number of Swedish small firms (less than 200 employees) with production abroad has quadrupled (Table 2.13).

Table 2.13. Number of Swedish small MNF with production units abroad.

Year	1965	1970	1974	1978	1986	1990	1994
Number of firms	8	7	9	15	18	23	32

Source: IUI surveys 1965, 1970, 1974, 1978, 1986, 1990 and 1994.

Similarly, export performance differs quite markedly among the three groups of firms. On average, large Swedish firms exported between 65 and 70 percent of their production in 1994, while exports by Swedish SMEs account for approximately 20 percent of their total sales, with wide differences among firms within the SME group. The most important market is the European Union (EU), receiving between 65 to 80 percent of the SMEs' exports. In the beginning of the 1990s, the export share to EU has increased for SMEs in the late 1980s and beginning of the 1990s (Table 2.14).[20] This partly reflects that the massive FDI undertaken by Swedish MNFs during the 1980s into the EC has had a pull effect on exports from the domestically located subcontractors, and partly the greater

---

[20] Data is only available for medium-sized firms.

attention paid to, at that time, the expectation of a future integrated European market.

Table 2.14. The distribution of SME exports on different regions, percentage, 1988-1990 and 1993.

	EU*	Nordic countries (except Denmark)	Rest of the World
1988	59	17	24
1989	59	15	26
1990	64	16	20
1993	82	15	3

Source: Braunerhjelm (1991a), Carlsson and Braunerhjelm (1994).
Note: *With the exclusion of the Nordic countries.

Overall, and in accordance with earlier empirical studies and the theoretical approach emphasizing firm-specific assets, it seems as if firms with some unique capability or knowledge, have been most successful on the international market. More specifically, medium-sized firms, often subcontractors, are stuck with problems of a more structural character than small firms in general. They are more deeply involved in production of relatively simple components that do not require any particular skill or knowledge, largely dependent on Swedish MNFs, their internationalization degree is quite low, and they seem to lack the resources required to develop their inhouse R&D-capacity. In fact, the R&D-intensity fell between 1990 and 1993 (Carlsson and Braunerhjelm, 1994). The latter circumstance is also true for the smaller firms but, since their customers are more local, it is of less concern. Moreover, medium-sized firms employ by far the largest proportion of unskilled labor and also display a lower profit performance then the other groups. Their problems are further aggravated by their customers' attempt to outsource part of the R&D activities on subcontractors at the same time as reductions in prices are demanded. To embark on internationalization, or to move production into more specialized and sophisticated segments, constitute a very delicate tasks under these circumstances.

2.5 Concluding Remarks

Much of the 1950s and 1960s were characterized by the establishment of large scale production units, designed for mass production of standardized goods. Organization of production followed Tayloristic and Fordistic principles, resulting in bureaucratic and hierarchic structures. Strategies to develop and sustain the competitive edge of firms was predominantly geared to low costs while less attention was paid to differentiation and quality. This trend came to a halt in the late 1960s. Demand shifted towards more differentiated, high quality products. At the same, internationalization of production increased due to the dismantling of trade barriers, continued integration efforts, and the improved and less expensive transportation systems. This led to a stiffening and widening of competition to sectors formerly shielded from international competition. Hence, traditionally home market orientated firms in industrialized countries hence became more exposed to foreign competition.

The last two to three decades have also been characterized by an impressive revival of SMEs in terms of employment shares, creation of value added and profit levels. The specific strongholds of SMEs are customization and prompt deliveries, paired with flexibility and related services (Storey, 1994). Furthermore, smaller units are claimed to attain higher cost efficiency as well as having flatter, non-bureaucratic, organizations and highly motivated personnel (Pratten, 1991). As technologies during the last decades have been adapted to suit small scale production, SMEs are often better equipped to encounter heterogeneous and volatile demand with their closer and more direct links to the market. But new technology also imposes constraints on the SMEs due to increased demand for human capital encompassing the knowledge required to handle more advanced technology and the altered circumstances relating to internationalization.

Technological progress and intensified competition seem to be two factors that have influenced the development of novel production modes, i.e., networks (broadly defined), technological systems and alike production structures. Even though this indicate a disintegration of the traditional firm, such systems are built on close and frequent interaction, mutual dependence and confidence among the participants. Networks are claimed to increase flexibility, induce a higher sensitivity to the price mechanisms and to enhance learning. As networks, and network externalities, are judged to become strategically more important, they will also influence investment and entry patterns. Clustering is likely to occur (see Chapters 5 and 6) since the location of large customer firms will be more influenced by such non-traditional factors as the regional composition of firms, skill levels, education etc. In addition to the possibility of exploiting network externalities this tends to induce even SMEs to undertake FDI in certain areas. Examples are the clustering of biotech firms in the south of France, the textile industry in the north of Italy and the regional clustering of part of the engineering tool industry in Germany. From such regional clustering of specific capabilities and competencies, a pattern of regional comparative advantage is likely to emerge.

Most of this is promising for the future of small firms. Their flexibility enables swift reactions to changes in demand and, in addition, local presence often certifies that service and maintenance can be supplied adequately. As international competition intensifies, SMEs can exploit their strength of small, flat organizations and flexible organizations, promoting high "economies of learning". All these factors seem to be positive for SME production, although there are some caveats to this story. First, past evolution of SMEs is blurred by the fragmented knowledge on the birth and death of firms and its effect on the distribution of firm size. If mainly large enterprises exit from the market it would render the impression that SMEs increases. Related to this is the question of "externalization", networks and how subsidiaries are treated in the statistics. Further, it should be noted that the changes in size distribution are measured in terms of employment. Obviously, if a large firm substitutes labor for more capital intensive techniques, while production remains constant, it is hard to argue that the firm has diminished in size (Carlsson, 1992; Carlsson and Taymaz, 1992). Hence, employment measures should preferably be complemented with other measures.

LITERATURE

Andersson, T., T. Fredriksson and R. Svensson, 1996, *Multinational Restructuring, Internationalization and Small Economies*, London: Routledge.

Asanuma, B., 1991, Coordination between Production and Distribution in a Globalized Network of Firms: Assessing Flexibility Achieved in the Japanese Automobile Industry, *mimeo*, Presented at the conference "Japan in the Global Economy", The Stockholm School of Economics, Stockholm, Sweden.

Birch, D., 1979, *The Job Generation Process*, Cambridge: MIT University Press.

Birch, D., 1981, Who Creates Jobs?, *Public Interest*, Fall, 3-14.

Birch, D., 1987, *Job Generation in America*, New York: Free Press.

Braunerhjelm, P., 1990, *Svenska industriföretag inför EG 1992 - Planer och förväntningar*, (Swedish Industrial Firms Afore EC 1992 - Plans and Expectations), Stockholm: The Research Institute of Industrial Economics (IUI).

Braunerhjelm, P., 1991, Svenska underleverantörer och småföretag - Struktur, internationalisering och kompetens, (Swedish Subcontractors and SMEs - Specialization, Internationalization and Competence), *Research Report 38*, Stockholm: The Research Institute of Industrial Economics (IUI).

Braunerhjelm, P. and K. Ekholm, K., 1998, *The Geography of Multinational Firms*, Boston, Dordrecht and London: Kluwer Academic Publishers.

Burns, P. and J. Dewhurst, 1986, *Small Business in Europe*, London: MacMillan.

Cantwell, J. and S. Raddacio, 1990, The Growth of Multinationals and the Catching Up Effect, *Economic Notes*, 1, 15-27.

Carlsson, B., 1989, The Evolution of Manufacturing Technology and Its Impact on Industrial Structure: An International Study, *Small Business Economics*, 1, 21-37.

Carlsson, B., 1992, The Rise of Small Business: Causes and Consequences, in W.J. Adams, (ed.), *Singular Europe: Economy and Polity of the European Community After 1992*, Ann Arbor: University of Michigan Press.

Carlsson, B. and P. Braunerhjelm, 1994, *Teknologiska system och ekonomisk tillväxt (Technological Systems and Economic Growth)*, Bilaga 10 till Långtidsutredningen 1994 in SOU 1995:4, Stockholm: Allmänna förlaget.

Carlsson, B. and G. Eliasson, 1991, The Nature and Importance of Economic Competence, *CWRU and WP 294*, The Industrial Institute for Economic and Social Research (IUI).

Carlsson, B. and E. Taymaz, 1992, Flexible Technology and Industrial Structure in the US, *WP 92.08*, Case Western Reserve University.

Commission of the European Communities, 1992, *Enterprises in the European Community*, Luxembourg.

Evans, D., 1991, *Industry Dynamics and Small Firms In the United States*, Report for the US Small Business Administration, NERA, Cambridge, USA.

Johansson, D., 1997, *The Number and the Size Distribution of Firms in Sweden and Other European Countries*, Licentiate Dissertation in Economics, IUI WP No. 483, Stockholm: IUI.

Larouche, G., 1989, Petites et moyennes entreprises au Quebec: Organizations économique, croissance de l'emploi et qualité du travail, *mimeo*, Institut Internationales d'Études Sociales, Geneva, Switzerland.

OECD, *OECD Employment Outlook*, 1985.

Pratten, C., 1991, *The Competitiveness of Small Firms*, Cambridge: Cambridge University Press.

Sengenberger, W., G. Loveman and M. Piore, 1990, *The Re-emergence of Small Enterprises: Industrial Countries*, Geneva: ILO.

Storey, D., 1994, *Understanding the Small Business Sector,* London: Routledge.

Swedenborg, B., 1979, *The Multinational Operations of Swedish Firms. An Analysis of Determinants and Effects*, Stockholm: IUI.

Chapter 3

DOES KNOWLEDGE INVESTMENT INCREASE PROFITABILITY?

Empirical Evidence from Swedish Firms in the Engineering Industry[21]

3.1 Introduction

Although its importance was first recognized long ago, the role of knowledge in firm performance has recently been rediscovered as a key to economic prosperity. That goes for the micro level (Eliasson, 1990; Grant, 1991) as well as the macro level (Romer, 1986; Grossman & Helpman, 1991). Still, most economic models tend to ignore knowledge factors or classify them as residual effects. If knowledge is incorporated at all, it is generally restricted to R&D investments, although activities like organizational routines, education, networks, marketing, supporting systems, etc., all form the base of the knowledge stock of a firm or country (Nelson & Winter, 1982; Spencer & Valla, 1989; Porter, 1990). As pointed out by for instance Freeman (1994) "it is often unsatisfactory to use R&D expenditure statistics as a surrogate for all those activities at the level of the firm which are directed towards knowledge accumulation, technical change and innovation. We have measures of 'capital-intensity' and of 'energy-intensity', but not of 'knowledge-intensity'".

The purpose of this chapter is to conceptualize knowledge capital and to incorporate it into a simple model of the firm, from which hypotheses concerning the relation between profitability and knowledge capital will be derived and empirically tested. The analysis differs from previous research in that it introduces a stock variable that more closely corresponds to the theoretically derived concept of firm-specific assets. In addition to R&D-investments, it also comprises investments in marketing, education and software. The empirical analysis is based on a unique firm data set emanating from extensive surveys carried out by the Research Institute of Industrial Economics (IUI).[22]

The chapter is organized in the following way: The definition of knowledge capital is presented in the next section (section 3.2). A simple model of knowledge based, profit-maximizing firms is presented in section 3.3. The

---

[21] A version of this chapter has been published in the Revue d'Economie et Industrielle (1996).
[22] For a detailed description of the survey, see Braunerhjelm (1992).

hypotheses derived from the model are specified and empirically tested in section 3.4. Finally, the main results are summarized and some normative implications discussed (section 3.5).

3.2 Knowledge Capital

The importance of knowledge has been recognized in several fields of economic research, e.g. the theory of human capital, the impact of public goods, and the recent contributions to growth theory (Knight, 1921, 1944; McKenzie, 1959; Arrow, 1962; Kendrick, 1976; Griliches, 1979; Romer, 1986; Sala-i-Martin, 1990; Becker, 1994; Eliasson & Braunerhjelm, 1997). Yet, being an intangible good, most attempts to incorporate it explicitly into the production function as a factor of production have been frustrated. Despite the impressive theoretical achievements, empirical evidence remains quite scarce.

To assess the influence of knowledge on firm performance, a stock concept of such assets has to be developed. But investments related to knowledge assets are, in accordance with the existing legislation and conventions, booked directly on the firm's expense account. This means that empirical analyses run into considerable computational, definitional, and methodological problems since knowledge stocks have to be constructed. Furthermore, knowledge will always contain elements of tacitness related to entrepreneurial skill, luck and other non-measurable factors. Still, as argued by for instance Eliasson (1992), much of the same difficulties arise when investments in real capital are undertaken. Moreover, the growth of knowledge assets within firms strongly suggests that such assets cannot be omitted from economic analysis (Bryer, 1990).

One question addressed in the knowledge literature concerns the differences in profits between firms. Even within narrowly defined industries wide dispersions in profit rates can be found, violating the standard assumption of equalization of profits. Such differences have been shown to persist over long periods of time, and one cannot simply refer to them as temporary divergences from equilibrium (Shepherd, 1975; Chandler, 1990; Mueller, 1990). Scherer (1986) argues that firms that manage to build up a "reputational capital" can charge a premium due to such capital, or expand their customer base at a lower price compared to their competitors. Other studies confer the main explanations to collusion and structural entry barriers, particularly tariffs and market dominance (Bain, 1955; Collins & Preston, 1968; Shepherd, 1972; Demsetz, 1973; Porter, 1974; Weiss, 1974; Carter, 1978; Ravenscraft, 1983; Mueller, 1990). The persistent profit argument seems, however, to be at least partly based on wrongly specified models since most studies only consider surviving firms, i.e. they do not account for sample selection bias. Those firms that fail and exit do not show up in the data sets.

Somewhat surprising, less attention has been paid to the effects of investment in intangibles in explaining the incidence of profits across firms. One explanation is of course the lack of good data on accumulated investments in intangible knowledge assets such as R&D and marketing. The relatively few empirical studies that exists are predominantly based on industry data, where the applied lag distributions frequently are assumed identical across firms, and even industries. The conclusion from most of these studies is that a strong and rather immediate relationship exists between marketing and profitability (Boyer, 1974; Ayanian, 1975; Lambin, 1976; Comanor & Wilson, 1979). Block (1974) and Weiss (1974), however, report opposite findings. For R&D expenses, a positive effect has been found in most empirical studies, although it appears with a considerable lag (Branch, 1974; Ravenscraft-Scherer, 1982). But also here the evidence is ambiguous. For instance, Megna & Mueller (1991) finds weak support for R&D as an explanatory variable of profits.

With regard to the definition of knowledge there is at present no generally accepted definition of intangible capital, nor means of denominating it. "Knowledge capital" seems to be the most frequently used term, even though the literature also refers to "intangibles", "competence capital", and "soft capital," to name a few. Since knowledge alludes to abilities within the firm, both organizational and collective, as well as individual, we will adopt the following and somewhat more extensive definition of knowledge capital:

This definition is operationalized by accumulating costs earlier charged on the current cost account. Costs with short-run effects (less than one year) are not activated as asset values, and all assets are expressed at reproduction value. The firms in the survey have themselves identified the investments whose returns they have appropriated, i.e. the measure of knowledge stocks is a subjective one.

Knowledge capital of firms is defined as accumulated assets in R&D, marketing, software and education, where the returns are appropriated by the firms themselves.[23]

This definition is operationalized by accumulating costs earlier charged on the current cost account. Costs with short-run effects (less than one year) are not activated as asset values, and all assets are expressed at reproduction value. The firms in the survey have themselves identified the investments whose returns they have appropriated, i.e. the measure of knowledge stocks in a subjective one.

The chosen items that constitute knowledge capital are consistent with the definitions of intangible assets analyzed separately in other studies. They all have a close links with skills and new technology. In addition to the frequently imposed variables R&D and marketing, we also include investments in education and software. The motivation is that these knowledge categories have a direct bearing to knowledge content of the firm as an organizational entity, where part is codified and easily accessible to other economic agents whereas

---

[23] Becker (1994) refutes the idea that firms under-invest in training due to the risk that their employees may leave the firm. Instead, workers accept lower wages for training.

other parts have a more tacit nature and are appropriated by the firms themselves. In contrast to much of previous studies in this field, where knowledge is assumed homogenous across firms, or even across industries, the above definition emphasize the firm-specific aspect of knowledge capital.[24]

3.3 Model, Data and Hypotheses

3.3.1 A Simple Model of Knowledge Endowments and Firm Performance[25]

Suppose that the market structure in which firms operate is characterized by imperfect competition, while firms are assumed to be profit-maximizing and to employ regular production technologies. How successful firms are depend on to which extent they can differentiate their product from those of their competitors, a process in which the exploitation of their knowledge capital is crucial. The degree of differentiation, or uniqueness, generates temporary monopolies which shows up in higher profits.

Models incorporating intangible assets are generally based on either the assumption that such investments shifts a firm's demand function (Clarke, 1976; Megna & Mueller, 1991), or that intangibles act as a shift factor in the production function (Griliches, 1979; Romer, 1986). It is the latter approach that is adopted here. Profits, defined as residual revenues not distributed to labor and real capital, will be derived from this approach. We assume the following basic structure of production of a representative firm. All firms employ three factors of production, labor (L), capital (K) and a composite knowledge capital (H). Perfect competition prevails on the factor markets for capital and labor, while H is firm-specific, heterogenous, and contained within the firms. Such firm-specific knowledge capital (H) shapes and adds value to downstream production by differentiating it from other close varieties. Downstream activities employ homogeneous capital (K) and labor (L), on which knowledge capital—employed in upstream activities, e.g., R&D, marketing , etc.—acts as a shift-factor.[26]

---

[24] Grossman-Helpman (1991) use a similar approach, separating between specific technological information and general technological information.

[25] A more technical presentation of the model can be found in Appendix A.3.1.

[26] Already Knight (1921) objected to the idea that increasing returns to scale were external in all respects to firms.

3.3.2 Data

To acquire data on knowledge capital, normally not reported in the firm's annual reports, several methods are available. First, growth accounting can be utilized to isolate the impact of R&D on outputs.[27] Second, the stock of knowledge capital can be calculated by gathering information from the firms directly through interviews and questionnaires or in close collaboration with, the firms themselves. This is the approach taken here.[28] Of course, also this method can be claimed to be arbitrary and it is doubtlessly based on a subjective evaluation. However, the values are at least based on estimates coming directly from the firms, i.e. those who should be best at evaluating these values. Each value has been thoroughly checked in interviews with each of the participating firms.[29]

This method has some obvious advantages. First, we can disregard the lag-problem. At present, there is no consensus concerning the lag structure. For instance, in capitalizing R&D expenditures Terleckyj (1982) used a three-year lag, while Pakes & Schankerman (1984) and Griliches & Lichtenberg (1984) implemented a two-year lag. Several other lag structures are also used. Furthermore, we avoid the difficulties stemming from different assumptions with regard to the depreciation rate of R&D. Also here opinions differ. Terleckyj (1982) argues that the most reasonable results are obtained if no depreciation at all is assumed, while others claim that yearly depreciation is more likely to be around 20-30 percent (Pakes & Schankerman 1984). Related to this is the

---

[27] Growth accounting implies that the growth of inputs (k and l) is subtracted from the growth of output which yields the multi-factor productivity growth. It can be used to isolate the effect of R&D. Consider the following Cobb-Douglas production function (q), where all variables are expressed as percentage rate of change,

$$q - \alpha_1 k - \alpha_2 l = a + \alpha_3 r$$

Productivity growth is decomposed into a constant and the effect of R&D(=r). The underlying assumption is that each factor's contribution to output can be determined by multiplying its income share by its rate of growth, i.e. each input is taken to be paid exactly its marginal product.

[28] The question concerning knowledge capital was formulated in the following way: "Please quantify the firms accumulated assets in R&D, marketing, software and education, either by giving the value directly in Swedish krona, or as percent of fixed assets. Values should be calculated as accumulated investments in above categories, after depreciation and in repurchase prices."

[29] Information gathered through interviews has sometimes been claimed to be unscientific. Commenting on that controversy, Scherer (1986) makes an analog that medium-sized firms have to a limited number of customers which makes y to the difficulties that astronomists encountered in the 17th century in determining the shape of the planetary orbits. Kepler, unable to observe the planetary motions, assumed that they were circular. However, when he visited Tycho Brahe he could actually observe that the orbits were elliptical, which impelled Scherer to make the following remark; "If Kepler could have interviewed God about what laws of planetary motion He ordained, would he have refrained because it was unscientific? One doubts it."

problem of obtaining an estimate of the R&D-stock in real terms, where again there are numerous recommendations. In essence, what this tells us is that the calculations of R&D stocks are plagued by a number of difficulties which will, to varying degrees, insert errors into the estimates.[30]

3.3.3 Hypotheses

The empirical application will be based on the simple model outlined above. Rather than subjecting the model itself to a rigorous test, the basic hypothesis to be empirically tested is derived from the theoretical model. In particular, our analysis is constrained by the fact that our database alludes to one single year of observation. Heterogeneity, and free entry of firms, imply that in a given year firms are likely to be in different phases regarding their accumulation of knowledge. We therefore expect a positive relation between firms' endowment of knowledge (H) and their profitability. The intuitive explanation is the following: firms engage in product differentiation to maximize profits, whereby a firm's ability to undertake such differentiation depends on its accumulated skills and know-how, i.e. its knowledge stock. A larger knowledge stock is claimed to facilitate the integration of new technology into the firm's production process as well as the upgrading of its existing technology. Furthermore, knowledge as defined above, should improve the firm's possibility to respond to alterations in consumer preferences.

If there is no well-defined factor to appropriate the return to such knowledge, returns will show up as residual profits or Schumpeterian rent. On the other hand, if labor managed to appropriate all of the returns to knowledge, that would have a negative impact on the firm's profitability. Hence, we expect a negative relationship between costs of labor (W) and profitability.

A few control variables, where previous research has established a relation to profitability, will also be included into the empirical analysis. First, to attain a certain scale is often regarded as necessary in order for firms to become profitable. Thus, size (S)—measured in terms of labor or sales— is asserted to be positively related to profits. Furthermore, in small countries, large firms can be expected to be dependent on the international market to sustain profits. Therefore, in addition to exports (X), a size-weighted relationship between profits and exports (XL) will also be incorporated into the analysis.

Similarity, market power (POWER) has frequently been invoked to explain differences across firms in profitability. Market dominance allows monopoly pricing to a larger extent and is also an indication of how successful firms have been in impeding entry by other firms. Therefore we expect market power to be positively connected with profits. Finally, we control for productivity (LP) since

---

[30] For a survey of these problems, see the study by the US Department of Labor (1989).

in order to make profits, a firm's ability to differentiate its product must be parallelled by a productivity level which is comparable to its competitors.

3.4 Econometric Specifications and Results

The sample consists of 150 firms in the engineering industry (ISIC 38), randomly chosen by SCB (Sweden Statistics). Out of the 150 firms, 13 were excluded because of changes in production, exits, etc. The remaining 137 firms were compared against industry averages to make sure they constituted a representative selection. The data collection was undertaken by IUI, mainly through extensive surveys, and to some extent complemented by data from public sources. All data refers to 1990.

The endogenous variable is the firm's real profit margin (Π_i), defined as sales revenue minus total costs. In accordance with discussion above, and the theoretical model in section 3, the following general functional relationship is postulated:

$$\Pi_i = f(H,S,X,XL,POWER,LP,W)$$

All variables have been deflated by the consumer price index and divided by total capital to avoid problems of heteroscedasticity and to isolate them from effects of firm size. This implies that the dependent variable also can be interpreted as the real rate of return on total capital (ε_i). From correlation matrices there is no sign of multicollinearity. The hypotheses formulated above will be tested by applying OLS estimation to a logarithmic form of the profit-function,

$$\varepsilon_i^* = a + b_1 h_i + b_2 s_i + b_3(xl)_i + b_4 x_i + b_5 power_i + b_6(lp)_i - b_7 w_i + \eta \qquad (3.1)$$

where ε_i^* denotes the rate of return inclusive of the hidden unknown return to knowledge capital. The error term is expected to exhibit standard properties, $\eta \sim N(0,\sigma^2)$ and $E(\eta_i \eta_j) = 0$ for $i \neq j$.

The effect of knowledge (h) is tested by implementing predominantly stock variables.[31] Among these, SOFT1 refers to the stock of knowledge capital—as defined above—of firms, while the variable GR&D, defined as current R&D expenditure divided by the R&D-stock, denotes the growth in the R&D stock. Alternatively, the skill structure of firms (SKILL), which is a more commonly

---

[31] Some overlapping of current costs and capitalized items is inevitable. As noted by Griliches (1973), since the inputs of capital and labor includes the factors of production used in R&D, the social rate of return is beyond the private rate of return (see also Griliches and Lichtenberg, 1984).

used knowledge proxy, is implemented to see to what extent the explanatory power differs between these two variables.[32] As expected, several tests with flow variables failed to show any significance. Stock variables are preferred since the effects of building up current knowledge through, for instance, R&D appear with a significant lag and only a fraction of current expenditure will eventually add to the stock of knowledge. Size (s) measured as numbers of employees, sales, or assets were also included. In all cases they were found to be insignificantly connected to the rate of return. Although evidence is somewhat mixed, this is consistent with a number of other studies (Burns & Dewhurst 1986, Braunerhjelm 1991). Instead, size was used as a weight to test whether foreign sales increase in importance for profits as firms become larger,

$$b_x x, \text{ where } b_x = (b_{x1} + b_{x2}l)$$

where l and x refer to employees and exports, respectively. If the hypothesis is supported, the parameter of the size weighted exports (b_{x2}) should be significant, while it is more difficult to a priori attach any sign to b_{x1}. Market power (POWER), measured as the firm's percentage of total sales in the engineering industry, i.e. market share, was also included since previous studies claim it to be an important explanatory variable of high profits.

The costs of homogenous factors (w) were approximated by the firm's labor costs (including social costs). Finally, labor productivity (lp), defined as value added per employee was included as an explanatory variable. To some extent it also captures the type of production within the firm.[33] The expected signs of the explanatory variables are summarized in Table 3.1.

---

[32] The employees of the firms have been divided into five different skill categories. The variable SKILL refers to the second and the third category, i.e. specialists, technicians and employees in other service-oriented activities within the firm (see Braunerhjelm, 1992).

[33] Value added could also be used as a measure of a firm's knowledge endowment. The drawbacks are, however, that such values also incorporate effects of protectionism, regulations, etc. Furthermore, a cross-sectional study only includes data for one year. To be able to interpret value added as a knowledge variable, data would be required over the whole business cycle in order to adjust for peak values. The same problem does not arise with stock values which are more stable over time.

Table 3.1. Definition and expected signs of explanatory variables.

Explanatory variables	sign
SOFT1, amount of knowledge capital per labor unit	+
SKILL, percentage of skilled employees	+
GR&D, current R&D expenses divided by the R&D stock	+
X, absolute value of exports	+/-
XL, absolute value of exports weighted by labor	+
W, total labor costs	-
LP, labor productivity defined as value-added per employee	+
POWER, percentage sale of total domestic sale	

The results are shown in Table 3.2.[34] In the first model (Model 1), where the implemented knowledge stock is SOFT1, all variables are significant at the 1 percent level, with the exception of the growth of the R&D stock (significant at the 5 percent level). Only the market power variable is insignificant. This is probably related to the relatively small size of the sample in relation to the total engineering industry. Hence, there is strong support for a positive relationship between firms' profitability and the stock of knowledge capital.

Exports by large firms have the expected positive sign and are significant while "pure" exports display a negative impact on profits. This could be interpreted as follows: large firms are dependent on exports to sustain profits, while small firms, experiencing lower profits as they engage in export activities, do not possess the competence required to operate on the international markets.[35]

In the second model (Model 2) the knowledge stock has been replaced by a more mainstream knowledge variable, i.e. SKILL, which captures the share of highly educated employees within the firms. It is also significant, albeit at a lower level. This is not surprising, considering that it is a less encompassing concept of knowledge, as compared to the variable SOFT1. Remaining variables

---

[34] The different items composing knowledge capital (see definition) were also exposed to a principal component analysis with no improved result. A Hausman test, undertaken to control for the causality between profits and knowledge capital, showed no significance for the opposite causality.

[35] This is in accordance with interview results from smaller firms where it was claimed that the export market was used as a dumping market for production surpluses (Braunerhjelm, 1991).

Table 3.2. Profitability and knowledge capital, 1989.

Independent variables	Dependent variable, profitability	
	Model 1	Model 2
Intercept	.37 (.15)	.35 (.13)
SKILL		.21* (1.67)
SOFT1	.16*** (2.61)	
GR&D	.09** (2.12)	.02 (.64)
X	-2.84*** (-8.99)	-2.86*** (-8.79)
XL	2.82*** (8.80)	2.87*** (8.70)
W	-2.32*** (-8.50)	-2.42*** (-8.21)
LP	2.77*** (8.77)	2.88*** (8.91)
POWER	.21 (.99)	.23 (.96)
Adj.R^2	.70	.68
F-value	23.3	21.4
DF	129	128

Note: The t-statistics are within brackets.* = 10 percent significance level, ** = 5 percent significance level, *** = 1 percent significance level

seem robust with respect to parameter estimate and significance level, with the exception of growth of the R&D stock which fail to reach significance. For both models the adjusted R^2 values, as well as the F-values, are quite satisfactory.

3.5 Concluding Remarks

In the above analysis, we have studied the relation between firm profitability and knowledge stocks, implementing a unique IUI data-set which captures firm-specific assets in a more direct way than traditional data on R&D and marketing. A static approach was pursued since in the empirical analysis we were confined to a cross-section data-set of firms in the engineering sector for a given point in time. Of course, a more dynamic approach would have been preferable considering the dynamic nature of knowledge itself. Despite the limitation of the model, we believe that the analysis yields valuable insights as regards the role of knowledge in firm performance.

Noteworthy and strong support is found for a positive relationship between profitability and the stock of knowledge capital on one hand, and profitability and exports in large firms on the other. The first findings contrasts with, for instance, the results reported by Megna & Mueller (1991). The second result highlight the heavy dependence of large firms on foreign markets to sustain profit levels. For smaller firms an opposite relation is indicated; exports tend to lower profits. No statistical significance was found for a relationship between size and profitability.

If we believe that profits over time transfer into positive welfare effects through e.g. wealth accumulation, higher investments and wages, then it is obvious that economic policies should be designed to encourage knowledge accumulation. Such policies could however only lay down the basic prerequisites for firms by providing advanced high-quality education, competitive infrastructures and communication systems. The firms themselves, through their acquired knowledge and in competition with other firms, have to determine the allocation and composition of their knowledge capital.

LITERATURE

Arrow, K., 1962., The Economic Implications of Learning by Doing, *Review of Economics and Statistics*, Vol. 80, pp. 155-173.

Ayanian, R., 1975, Advertising and Rate of Return, *Journal of Law and Economics*, Vol. 18, pp. 479-506.

Bain, J., 1955, *Barriers to New Competition*, Harvard University Press, Cambridge, Ma.

Becker, G., 1994, *Human Capital*, 4th edition, Columbia University Press, New York.

Block, H., 1974, Advertising and Profitability: A Reappraisal, *Review of Economics and Statistics*, Vol. 55, pp. 541-548.

Boyer, K., 1974, Informative and Goodwill Advertising, *Review of Economics and Statistics*, Vol. 56, pp. 541-548.

Branch, B., 1974, Research and Development Activities and Profitability: A Distributed Lag Analysis, *Journal of Political Economy*, Vol. 82, pp. 999-1013.

Braunerhjelm, P., 1991, Svenska underleverantörer och småföretag i det nya Europa (Prospects for Swedish Subcontractors and SMEs in a New Europe), *Research Report 38*, IUI, Stockholm.

Braunerhjelm, P., 1992, Competence, Capacity and Competence; A Description of Complementary IUI Firm Survey of Small and Large Firms and of Subcontractors, in Albrecht, J. et al., Moses Database, *Research Report No 40*, IUI, Stockholm.

Braunerhjelm, P., 1997, On the Role of Knowledge Capital in Firm Performance, *Revue d'Economie et Industrielle,* No. 81, 1997, pp. 9-22.

Bryer, R., 1990, Economic Income is Dead! Long Live Economic Income? Accounting for the Controversy Over the Good-Will in the UK, *Research Paper 30*, Warwick Business School, England.

Burns, P., Dewhurst, J., 1986, *Small Business in Europe*, MacMillan, London.

Carter, J., 1978, Collusion, Efficiency, and Antitrust, *Journal of Law and Economics*, Vol. 21, pp. 435-444.

Chandler, A., 1990, *Scale and Scope*, Harvard University Press, Cambridge, Ma.

Clarke, D., 1976, Econometric Measurement of the Duration of Advertising Effects on Sales, *Journal of Marketing Research*, Vol. 13, pp. 345-357.

Collins, N., Preston, L., 1968, *Concentration and Price-Cost Margins in Manufacturing Industries*, University of California Press, Berkeley.

Comanor, W., Wilson, T., 1979, The Effect of Advertising on Competition: A Survey, *Journal of Economic Literature*, Vol. 17, pp. 453-476.

Demsetz, H., 1973, Industry Structure, Market Rivalry, and Public Policy, *Journal of Law and Economics*, Vol. 16, pp. 1-9.

Eliasson, G., 1990, The Firm as a Competent Team, *Journal of Economic Behavior and Organization*, Vol.13, pp. 275-298.

Eliasson, G., 1992, The Moses Model - Database and Applications, in Albrecht,

J., et al, Moses Database, *Research Report 40*, IUI, Stockholm.

Eliasson, G., Braunerhjelm, P, 1997, Human Embodied Capital and Firm Performance, in Eliasson, G., (Ed.), *The Microeconomic Foundations of Economic Growth*, Michigan University Press, forthcoming.

Freeman, C., 1994, The Economics of technical Change, *Cambridge Journal of Economics*, Vol. 18, pp. 463-514.

Grant, R., 1991, *Contemporary Strategy Analysis*, Basil Blackwell, Oxford.

Griliches, Z., 1973, Research Expenditure and Growth Accounting, in Williams, B., (ed.), *Science and Technology in Economic Growth*, John Wiley & Sons, New York.

Griliches, Z., 1979, Issues in Assessing the Contribution of Research and Development to Productivity Growth, *The Bell Journal of Economics*, Vol. 10, pp. 92-116.

Griliches, Z., Lichtenberg, F., 1984, R&D and Productivity and the Industry Level: Is There Still a Relationship?, in Griliches, Z., (ed.), *R&D, Patents and Productivity*, University of Chicago Press, Chicago.

Grossman, G., Helpman, E., 1991, *Innovation and Growth in a Global Economy*, MIT Press, Cambridge, Ma.

Hayek, J., 1945, The Use of Knowledge in Society, *American Economic Review*, Vol. 35, pp. 520-30.

Kendrick, J., 1976, *The Formation and Stock of Total Capital*, Columbia University Press, New York.

Knight, F., 1921, *Risk, Uncertainty, and Profit*, Houghton Mifflin, Boston.

Lambin, J., 1976, *Advertising, Competition, and Market Conduct in Oligopoly Over Time*, North-Holland, Amsterdam.

McKenzie, L., 1959, On the Existence of General Equilibrium for a Competitive Market, *Econometrica*, Vol. 27, pp. 54-71.

Megna, P., Mueller, D., 1991, Profit Rates and Intangible Capital, *Review of Economics and Statistics*, Vol. 73, pp. 632-642.

Mueller, D., 1986, *Profits in the Long Run*, Cambridge University Press, Cambridge, Ma.

Nelson, S., Winter, D., *An Evolutionary Theory of Economic Change*, Harvard University Press, Cambridge, Ma.

Pakes, A., Schankerman, M., 1984, The Rate of Obsolescence of Patents, Research Gestation Lags and the Private Rate of Return to Research Resources, in Griliches, Z., (ed.), *Patents and Productivity*, Chicago University Press, Chicago.

Porter, M., 1974, Consumer Behavior, Retailer Power, and Market Performance in Consumer Good, *Review of Economics and Statistics*, Vol. 56, pp. 419-436.

Porter, M., 1990, *The Competitive Advantage of Nations*, MacMillan, London.

Ravenscraft, D., 1983, Structure-Profit Relationship at the Line of Business and Industry Level, *Review of Economics and Statistics*, Vol. 65, pp. 22-31.

Ravenscraft, D., Scherer, F., 1982, The Lag Structure of Returns to Research and Development, *Applied Economics*, December, pp. 603-620.

Romer, P., 1986, Increasing Returns and Economic Growth, *American Economic Review*, Vol. 94, pp. 1002-1037.

Sala-i-Martin, X., 1990, Lecture Notes on Economic Growth, *WP 3563 and 3564*, NBER, Cambridge.

Scherer, F., 1986, On the Current State of Knowledge in Industrial Organization, in de Jong, H., Shephard, W., (eds.), *Mainstreams in Industrial Organization*, Martinus Nijhoff Publishers, Dordrecht.

Shepherd, W., 1972, The Elements of Market Structure, *Review of Economic and Statistics*, Vol. 54, pp. 23-57.

Shepherd, W., 1975, *The Treatment of Market Power*, Columbia University Press, New York.

Spencer, R., Valla, J.-P., 1989, The Internationalization of the Industrial Firm: An International Development Network Approach, in Luostarainen, R., (ed.), *Dynamics of International Business*, Proceedings of the XV Conference of the European Business Association, Helsinki.

Terleckyj, N., 1982, R&D and US Industrial Productivity in the 1970's, in Sahel, D., (ed.), *The Transfer and Utilization of Technical Knowledge*, Lexington Books, Lexington.

US Department of Labor, 1989, The Impact of Research and Development on Productivity Growth, Bureau of Labor Statistics, *Bulletin 2331*, Washington D.C.

Weiss, L., 1974, The Concentration-Profit Relationship and Antitrust, in Goldschmid, H. , Mann, H. and Weston, J., (eds.), *Industrial Concentration: The New Learning*, Little & Brown, Boston.

APPENDIX TO CHAPTER 3

Assume that all firms organize production by means of identical Cobb-Douglas technologies,

$$Q_i = AK_i^{1-\alpha}L_i^{\alpha}H_i^{\gamma} \tag{A3.1}$$

$$0 < \alpha,\gamma < 1$$

where L refers to labor, K stands for physical capital and H represents a composite knowledge capital. The restriction on γ is imposed to assert that firms cannot handle unlimited amounts of H, i.e. decreasing returns to H is postulated. The production function Q is hence assumed to be linearly homogenous in capital and labor, but to exhibit limited increasing returns to scale with regard to all factors.

As modeled, the production function is strongly separable, implying that it can be divided into a constant returns to scale part ($V_i = AK_i^{1-\alpha}L_i^{\alpha}$) and an increasing returns to scale part H_i^{γ}. Profit (Π) is then defined as

$$\Pi_i = P(V_iH_i^{\gamma}) - W_iV_i - R_iH_i \qquad \geq 0 \tag{A3.2}$$

where the unit costs of the linearly homogenous input aggregate (V_i) is denoted W_i while R_i represents the reward to each firm's knowledge capital H_i.[36] If H_i were a well-defined production factor within the firm, all residual profits (R_i) would be appropriated by that factor. Here it could be interpreted as the returns to owners or to entrepreneurial skill, frequently disregarded in economic models. It must be non-negative since firms cannot operate at negative profits.

Profit maximizing can be viewed as a two-step procedure. First, the optimal quantities of capital and labor are determined for given prices and a given stock of H_i, where profit is known to be zero. Thereafter, profits are maximized with respect to H_i, which is the step we focus on here. The equilibrium stock of knowledge capital for firm i is calculated by maximizing equation A3.2 subject to the restrictions in equation A3.1. Hence, differentiating profits with respect to H_i, yields the first order condition[37]

$$\Pi_{i,h} \equiv P\gamma H_i^{\gamma-1}V_i = R_i \tag{A3.3}$$

---

[36] In general, if a constant return to scale technology prevails, the cost function can be written as $c(w,y) = yc(w,1)$ which is utilized in equation A3.2.

[37] Subscripts denote partial derivatives, except for numbers (or t) that refer to periods, or i, which refers to firm i.

or, by (A3.1) and the definition of V_i

$$\gamma Q = r_i H_i \tag{A3.4}$$

$(r_i = R_i/P)$

implying that knowledge capital is employed until the marginal contribution of additional H equals the marginal (real) return demanded by the firms' owners, which is either distributed to owners or show up as profits.

The second order condition implies falling returns to H after some optimum stock of knowledge capital is reached,

$$\Pi_{i,hh} = (1-(1/\gamma))P_i V_i H^{\gamma-2} \quad < 0 \tag{A3.5}$$

which is unambiguously negative since $0 < \gamma < 1$. Consequently, the marginal effect of knowledge investments peters out and at some stage goes to zero.

Chapter 4

HOW IS KNOWLEDGE CAPITAL RELATED TO FIRM SIZE AND INTERNATIONALIZATION? [38]

4.1 Introduction

Sunk costs have long been recognized as a key determinant as regards the size distribution of firms and, consequently, the market structure. According to the traditional "structuralist" view, market structure and the degree of concentration is determined by different entry barriers, such as R&D and marketing expenditures (Bain, 1949 and 1955; Lall, 1980). As suggested by Sutton (1991), we can think of these expenditures "as sunk costs incurred with a view to enhancing consumers' willingness to pay for the firm's product(s)" (Sutton, 1991, pp. 7-8).[39] Hence, in order for firms to develop, sustain, and finance such costs, it has been claimed necessary to reach a certain critical scale in production. Empirically this view has also received some support (Greenhalg, 1991; Kravis and Lipsey, 1992).[40]

More recently, the question of whether sunk costs are endogenously or exogenously determined has been addressed. A simplistic description of the mechanism separating endogenous from exogenous sunk costs imply that in the former case sunk costs—and the firm—tend to grow in proportion with the size of the market. This is held to primarily be the case for firms with extensive outlays on R&D and marketing expenditures. As these firms increase their sunk costs in response to market growth, thereby preserving their market share and their profits, the market structure remain relatively invariant to changes in markets size (Sutton, 1991; Schmalensee, 1986 and 1992). This has been shown to hold for a surprisingly large number of different oligopoly models, irrespective of which type of game that is pursued (Sutton, 1991).

In a parallel strand of economics, which is also preoccupied with the impact

---

[38] For an extended version, see Braunerhjelm (1999).
[39] The difference between fixed costs and sunk costs is "one of degree, not of nature" (Tirole, 1994). One distinction is based on the length of the period that the costs are incurred. Fixed costs are the claimed to appear in the short- to medium-run, while sunk costs cannot be recouped and produce a stream of benefits over a longer term.
[40] For a review of this literature, see Cohen and Levin (1989). Although most studies confer a positive connection between concentration and R&D, some end up with the opposite conclusion. For instance, on firm level, Cohen and Movery (1987) find no positive connections between size and R&D-intensities. The alleged causality from size to R&D has rightly been criticized on grounds that a simultaneous relationship between firm size and R&D-expenditures is more likely to prevail (Dasgupta and Stiglitz, 1980; Caves, 1996; Fors, 1997).

of outlays on sunk costs and firm growth, a somewhat different perspective is taken. Here, the explicit condition for growth in terms of expanding sales into foreign markets, is claimed to be access to some firm-specific assets, originating in sunk costs in R&D, marketing, etc (Dunning, 1977; Helpman and Krugman, 1985; Markusen, 1995). Also here empirical evidence are ample (Caves, 1996).

One fundamental difference between the two models originate in their different assumptions as regards the settings in which firms operate. In the endogenous sunk cost model, a closed economy type of world is implicitly assumed to exist. Hence, entry can only occur through incumbent firms. Furthermore, the way these models are designed, i.e. different forms of oligopoly markets in a closed economy, make entry less probable. The internationalization model embark from an entirely different view of the world. Also in this case are markets characterized by imperfect competition, however, firms grow by entering foreign markets. And to carry the additional costs of serving foreign markets, either through foreign direct investments or through exports, firms incur sunk costs in R&D and marketing which is used to differentiate their goods from those of their competitors, thereby allowing a higher mark-up on prices. The models have in common that they assume that sunk costs can indeed shift the demand curve for the firm's product.

The purpose of this chapter is to examine which one of these seemingly opposing hypotheses that can be empirically supported. To achieve this end, we will implement firm data for a narrowly defined industry (engineering). Hence, we will consider a market structure that is somewhat wider then the strict oligopoly case. In the first part of the analysis we will examine whether firm size constitutes a critical factor in explaining the relative level of firms' sunk costs. Firms defined as large today have a growth process behind them.[41] If sunk costs are endogenous, i.e. if they increase in proportion to the size of the market, we would expect sunk costs to be of approximately the same relative magnitude, e.g., in relation to sales, irrespective of the firm's size. On the other hand, if the relative level of sunk costs differ across firms of different size, that tend to cast some doubts on the endogenous sunk cost hypothesis.[42]

Second, we will investigate how sunk costs, when we control for the size of the firms, influence entry into foreign markets. Such entry, or internationalization, can take different forms depending on economies of scale (at the firm or plant level), the level of trade costs, and the risk of being exposed to "opportunistic" behavior (Hymer, 1960; Williamson, 1975; Brainard, 1993). Here we will only consider internationalization defined in terms of export-intensity, while

---

[41] In essence, we are assuming that similar firms should react similarly to external shocks, as an enlargement of the market (cf Dixit, 1989).

[42] That the level of sunk ousts is smaller in smaller firms have found some support in for instance studies by Cabral (1995) and Gilbert (1989),claiming that this reduces the eventual costs of failed entry. Mansfield (1962), Dunne, Roberts and Samuelson (1989) and Mata (1994), conclude that a negative relation exists between firm growth and firm size, i.e. rejecting Gibrat's Law.

controlling for the effect of previously established foreign affiliates. If sunk costs has a positive effect on entry on foreign markets through exports, then taking that into account, the market structure in foreign markets will also change.

There are of course numerous factors that interact to determine the export performance by firms. Most prevalent among those are changes in relative prices. However, since we are focusing on a cross-examination of Swedish firms belonging to the same industry, this restriction should not be a cause of great concern since relative price changes vis-à-vis the world is likely to affect the included firms symmetrically. We also disregard factors like supplier structures, strategic considerations, etc., that may motivate firms to entry foreign markets.

The empirical analysis will be based on a firm data set for the year 1990 covering 137 Swedish firms in the engineering industry. In order to grasp the interrelations between sunk costs in firm-specific assets, size and internationalization, it is necessary to pin down the analysis to the sub-industry level. The data-set contain unique information on a stock variable representing accumulated sunk costs in firm-specific assets. In contrast to traditional stock measures, normally restricted to capitalized values of former R&D-expenditure, the extended definition applied here also incorporate investments in marketing and education. Both ordinary least square regression techniques, and methods allowing for a censored dependent variable, will be implemented. In the latter regressions, some of the estimations have been undertaken in the form of a recursive system. A censored dependent variable estimation technique implies that problems of selection bias can be avoided in the estimations of internationalization, where the dependent variable frequently takes on a value of zero.

This chapter is organized in the following way. Section 4.2 outlines the model and presents the hypotheses to be tested. The following section 4.3, contains the results of the econometrics analysis. Finally, the main results are summarized and discussed in section 4.4. A detailed description of the econometrics model can be found in the appendix.

4.2 Data and Hypotheses

After a brief presentation of the data, we present the hypotheses as regards the relation between firms' endowment of firm-specific assets per employee, i.e. their relative sunk cost, and firm size. Thereafter we define the variables invoked in explaining firms internationalization.

4.2.1 Data

The data were collected directly from a random sample of Swedish firms in the engineering sector through surveys and interviews for the year 1990. The selection procedure was performed by Sweden Statistics.[43] The data-set contains detailed information on sales, costs, skill-structure, investments, assets, and foreign production capacity. Mergers, other forms of exit, and altered production, meant that the original sample of 150 firms shrank to 137 firms. The size distribution of the sample is illustrated in Table 1. The key variable used in the analysis below is however the firms' level of sunk costs in firm-specific assets, defined as a stock variable. As shown in Eliasson & Braunerhjelm (1998), the market places no value on such firm-specific assets, hence they are indeed sunk costs. Not only are they derived from investments in R&D, but also in marketing and education. This should give a more accurate estimate of sunk costs, since R&D is just one component of such costs. This variable is operationalized by accumulating expenses on the current cost account, where costs associated with short-run effects (less than one year) are excluded and all values are after depreciation and at reproduction costs.[44]

Table 4.1. The size distribution of firms in the sample.

Size (numbers of employees)	Share of firms, percentage
< 100	38.4
100 - 200	21
200 - 500	18
> 500	22.6
Total	100

[43] The selection procedure was restricted in the following way: Firms having less than 20 employees was excluded on the basis that they would have negligible sunk costs in firm-specific assets as defined above. In addition, the size segments <100 employees, 100-500 employees, and >500 employees, should all contain at least 30 firms each (i.e., 20 percent). A somewhat finer classification level is used in Table 4.1. The questionnaire is available on request.

[44] Of course, also this method can be claimed to be arbitrary and it is doubtlessly based on a subjective evaluation. However, the values are at least based on estimates coming directly from the firms, i.e. those who should be best at evaluating these values. I our view, this method is superior to the one suggested by for example Lambson and Jensen (1998), using gross book value of property, plant and equipment. Each value used in the current analysis has been thoroughly checked in interviews with each of the 137 firms. The question was formulated in the following way: "Please quantify the firms accumulated assets in R&D, marketing and education, either by giving the value directly in Swedish krona, or as percent of fixed assets. Values should be calculated as accumulated investments in above categories, after depreciation and in repurchase prices."

4.2.2 Hypotheses

Sunk Costs and Firm Size

In the first part of the econometrics analyses, we will examine the relationship between the level of sunk costs in firm-specific knowledge assets, and the size of the firm. As regards the size variable, it is not self-evident which measure to use. The accuracy of traditional size variables, like the numbers of employees or assets, have become less apparent due to the emergence of new modes of organizing production. Networks, informal contracts, etc., tend to make the boundaries of the firm less distinct. Similarly, the asset side in the balance sheet is affected by novelties in the way investments are financed. For instance, if firms prefer to lease a large part of their equipments and housing, such assets will never show up in the balance sheet. However, the correlation between the different size measures we have (total turnover, total assets, and employment) is extremely high in our sample (all of the correlation coefficient exceeds .98), and we have chosen to implement the number of employees (L) as our size measure.

The remaining variables used in the regressions are the skill composition of the labor force, profits, production capacity abroad, the firms' production technology, and productivity. We will now motivate the implementation of each of these variables.

In the international business literature it is often argued that foreign affiliate production enable a firm to "tap" the host region of its specific and localized knowledge content (Zander, 1995). We have therefore added a variable that captures the respective firm's share of foreign production capacity in relation to its domestic production capacity, measured as the distribution of fixed assets between foreign and domestic production units (FUT). Hence, a higher share of foreign production is expected to contribute positively to a firm's relative level of sunk costs.

We also control for the capital intensity, or production technology, by inserting a variable defined as fixed assets per employee (CAP). High capital-intensity (CAP) is assumed to reflect more process, or raw material based production within the engineering industry, where firm-specific assets, as defined above, plays a less important role and hence a negative connection vis-à-vis firm-specific assets is hypothesized. We also include labor productivity (PROD), which is assumed to capture the quality and efficiency of labor, organizational skills, etc., after having controlled for the firm's capital-intensity. We expect a high labor productivity to be positively connected to the level of sunk costs in firm-specific assets.[45]

The skill-structure of firms' employees (S) is—for obvious reasons—also implemented as an explanatory into the regressions. The data-set contains information on the skill of employees divided into five different categories, based on the employees position within the firms, not their formal education. The skill variable is defined as the share of the two most skilled categories out of total employees in the Swedish units, and a positive impact on the dependent variable is expected.

Finally, in order to investigate whether a non-linear relationship prevails between firm-specific assets and size, we have included a quadratic size variable (QuadL). We have no a priori assumption about the sign of this variable. However, a negative sign implies that the influence of size on firms' endowments of firm-specific assets is diminishing, while a positive sign implies that larger firms exert a stronger impact on the accumulation of firm-specific assets.

Foreign Entry, Sunk Costs, and Firm Size: the Hypotheses

Turning to firms' internationalization, the analysis focusses on the influence of sunk costs in firm-specific assets (SC*) on entry into foreign markets through exports. Particularly, the objective is to examine whether the coefficient of sunk costs can be significantly distinguished from zero as we estimate the determinants of firms' foreign entry, controlling for size. A maintained assumption is that firms operate on markets characterized by imperfect competition, where firm-specific assets is assumed necessary in order for firms to differentiate their goods from close substitutes. The alternative hypothesis is hence that sunk costs in FSA*, as defined above, have a positive effect on the firm's export-intensity.[46]

The following control variables, all contained in the vector Z, are implemented in the regressions. Since firm-specific assets may also promote foreign entry through investments in other countries, we will control for the effect of foreign production capacity (FUT) on the firm's export-intensity.[47] Production units abroad may influence the export-intensity of firms in two conceivable ways. First, it can increase exports through a deeper integration across production units

---

[45] Jovanovic (1982) introduce a positive connection between productivity (efficiency) and the value of the firm, while other studies claim that sunk costs translate into higher firm value (Lambson and Jensen, 1998), suggesting an indirect link between sunk costs in firm-specific assets and productivity.

[46] Support for this is also provided by Teece (1982), and Ollinger, Fernandez & Cornejo (1998).

[47] See also Caves (1971), Swedenborg (1979), Dunning (1980), Lall (1980), Hirsch and Biaouhi (1985), Hughes (1985), Greenhalg (1991), and Kravis and Lipsey (1992). These studies embrace exports as well as foreign direct investment.

located in different countries. Consequently, in this case the probability of a firm having export should increase if it has foreign subsidiaries. Second, it can also be argued that foreign affiliates replace production in domestic units, implying a negative link between exports from the Swedish based plants and foreign production (Svensson, 1996). It is therefore difficult to a priori assign the effect of foreign production capacity on the export-intensity of firms.

For a small open economy with a limited domestic market, we expect a positive impact of firm size (SIZE) on the firm's exports.[48] For a similar reason, we conjecture that higher capital-intensity in production (CAP), reflecting process- and raw material intensive production, will augment exports. The production volumes required to exploit economies of scale on the plant level can only be attained through exports.[49] Finally, labor productivity (PROD), defined as above, is supposed to enhance the competitiveness of the firm and to positively influence the firms' export-intensity.

In two separate estimations, we have included proxies for sunk costs in firm-specific assets directly into the Tobit function. The first proxy, i.e. the skill composition of the firms' employees (S), was defined as exogenous in Model I, which means that we do not have take into consideration eventual endogenic problems, and can estimate the Tobit function directly. We also implement the sum of current expenditures on R&D and marketing per employee, denoted SPEC, as an alternative proxy. The aim is to examine whether a flow variable yields results that differs from the stock value of FSA, and to what extent these proxies support the findings of the first estimation using stock values. The definitions and expected signs of the explanatory variables are summarized in Table 4.2.

4.3 Results

Starting with the relation between sunk costs in firm-specific assets and size, the results are shown in Table 4.3.[50] In the first estimation (Model Ia), the size variable has the expected sign but fails to attain significance. Among the control variables, the skill structure of employees is shown to have the strongest influence on the firm's level of sunk costs. Also profitability has a positive impact on FSA, albeit much weaker. The other control variables, that is, productivity, capital-intensity, and foreign production capacity, all fail to attain

---

[48] A strong positive relationship of size on exports is found in most studies. For an overview, see Miesenbock (1989).
[49] In the theoretical literature scale economies on the firm level favors foreign direct investment (FDI), while scale effects on the plant level is more likely to promote exports. Important in this context is the interaction between economies of scale and trade costs (see Brainard, 1993).
[50] The econometrics model is presented in the appendix.

statistical significance. As shown in Model Ib, the overall explanatory power of the regression is substantially reduced if we omit the variable capturing the skill composition of firms. Moreover, size then appears to have a weak positive influence on FSA, while profitability become negative and insignificant. Instead labor productivity is shown to have a significantly positive effect on the dependent variable, probably due to that some of the effects contained in the omitted skill variable is then captured by the productivity variable. Moreover, capital-intensive production technologies seem to exert a negative impact on the accumulation of FSA.

Table 4.2. Definitions and expected signs of explanatory variables.

Exogenous variables, firm level data	Definitions	Expected sign
Sunk costs in firm-specific assets	FSA, accumulated stock of investments in R&D, marketing and education per employee	+
Size	L, total domestic employment	+
Quadratic size	QuadL, quadratic value of L	?
Skill structure of employees	S, the percentage share of the two most qualified categories of employees	+
Productivity	PROD, value-added per employee	+
Capital-intensity	CAP, fixed assets per employee	+/-
R&D and marketing outlays	SPEC, current expenditure on R&D and marketing per employee	+
Production abroad	FUT, percentage of fixed assets abroad	?

The insignificance of size in the first regression (Model Ia), may be due to a non-linear relationship between size and the firm's endowment of firm-specific

Table 4.3. Sunk costs in firm-specific assets and size (1990).

Method = OLS	MODEL I (Dependent variable = firm-specific assets/employee)		
Independent variables	Model Ia	Model Ib	Model Ic
INTERCEPT	.004 (.14)	-4.63*** (-10.17)	.003 (.10)
L	2.1E-7 (.76)	7.0 E-6* (1.82)	1.7 E-6** (2.21)
PROD	-.18 (1.21)	6.69*** (3.41)	-.17 (-1.12)
CAP	.003 (.08)	-1.30*** (-2.67)	-.003 (-.09)
FUT	-7.3 E-7 (-.11)	-.001 (-.68)	-7.1 E-6 (-.96)
S	.37*** (5.69)	--	.34*** (5.12)
QuadL			-3.1 E-10** (-2.07)
F-value	7.81	4.17	7.47
Adj. R²	.23	.11	.25
No of Observations	134	134	134

Note: ***, ** and * indicate significance at 1, 5 and 10 percent respectively, t-values in parenthesis.

assets. It could be that firms of different size are inherently different. In the following estimation (Model Ic), we have therefore included a quadratic size variable to capture the presence of a non-linear relationship. As revealed in the estimation of Model Ic, the introduction of the quadratic variable has a substantial effect on the results. First, the size variable turns significant on the 5-percent level, implying that FSA is indeed increasing in size. However, as shown by the negative quadratic size variable, also significant at the 5-percent level, the impact of size is decreasing. The parameter value, being much smaller than for the size variable, implies that the decreasing effect is relatively limited. Hence, there seems to be a concave relationship between the size of the firm and the firm's endowment of FSA. This can be interpreted as if the often asserted ability of firms to handle knowledge is limited, i.e., the firm can only handle knowledge efficiently up to a given level. The inclusion of the quadratic size variable had little effect on the remaining control variables, as compared to estimation of Model Ia. Hence, firms serving a larger market will increase their relative outlays on sunk costs, however, at a decreasing rate.

To summarize, the results of the first regression (Model I) suggest that size—together with the skill structure—has a positive but diminishing impact on firms' relative endowments of sunk costs in FSA.[51] Hence, the coefficient of size is significantly separated from zero and we can reject the null hypothesis.

Turning to the firms degree of internationalization, Table 4.4 pictures the result of the Tobit estimations (i.e., the second step of Model II) of the impact of sunk costs in firm-specific assets (SC*) per employee on entry through exports. The Tobit equations are first estimated as a recursive system. Controlling for the effect of firm size, the strongest support is found for the SC*-variable, which is significant at the one-percent level (Model IIa). Both the variables capturing size and capital-intensive production technologies are found to have a (weak) positive impact on export-intensity. Furthermore, productivity has the expected positive impact and is significant, while the influence of profits contradicts our expectations, being significant and negative. The prevalence of foreign affiliate production capacity is negatively related to export-intensity, but fails to attain significance. Taken together, the results suggest that sunk costs in firm-specific assets has a strong and dominant effect on entry by firms on foreign markets through exports.

In the following two estimations (Model IIb and IIc), sunk costs in SC* have been replaced by current expenditure on R&D and marketing (SPEC) per employee, and the skill structure of the firms' employees (S), respectively. These variables have been inserted directly into the Tobit equation. The remaining control variables are identical to those in the first Tobit estimation. As can be seen in Table 4.4, both of these variables also attain significance in the Tobit estimations, implying that impact of sunk costs on entry through exports seems robust. However, much of the significance of the control variables vanish or is diminished. Furthermore, the coefficients for the proxies of sunk costs in FSA are also considerably lower. We therefore conclude that the stock measure seems to be the preferable proxy for sunk costs in firm-specific assets.

To conclude, the estimations provide evidence that the coefficient of sunk costs in firm-specific assets is significantly distinguished from zero, and also in this case we can reject the null hypothesis. Rather, sunk costs in firm-specific assets seems to be a means for the firm to grow by entering foreign markets, thereby expanding their sales.

---

[51] A Houseman test confirms that causality goes from the skill-structure of employees to firm-specific assets, not the other way.

Table 4.4. Internationalization, sunk costs in firms-specific assets, and size (1990).

Method = Tobit	Dependent variable = EXP/TS		
Independent variables	Model IIa (recursive system)	Model IIb	Model IIc
INTERCEPT	-.13* (-.08)	-.04 (.08)	-.13* (.08)
SC*	2.29*** (.39)		
SPEC		1.70*** (.39)	
S			.77*** (.16)
L	1.15 E-5 * (7.17 E-6)	1.81 E-5** (7.34 E-6)	2.02 E-5*** (7.10 E-6)
PROD	.57* (.32)	.51 (.35)	.30 (.36)
CAP	.12* (.07)	.06 (.08)	.11 (.08)
FUT	-1.21 E-4 (1.58 E-3)	-1.93 E-4 (1.66 E-4)	-1.97 E-4 (1.62 E-4)
Log lik.hood	20.26	25.11	25.83
No. of observations Left censored variables	134	134	137
	26	26	26

Note: Standard errors in parentheses. ***, ** and * indicate significance at 1, 5 and 10 percent respectively.

4.4 Concluding Remarks

In this paper we have attempted to shed light on the relation between sunk costs in firms-specific assets (FSA) and firm (market) size on the one hand, and sunk costs in FSA and entry on foreign markets through exports on the other hand. We have done that by confronting two hypotheses in the industrial organization literature that to some extent seem to contradict each other. Do firms expand their investments in sunk costs in proportion to an expansion of the market, or does the market expand for firms that incur higher expenditures on sunk costs? If the former was true, then we would expect firms of different size—i.e. irrespective of the size of the market they serve—to have approximately the same relative expenditure levels for sunk costs, e.g., per employee. On the other hand, if firms manage to shift the foreign demand curve for their products as they increase the level of sunk costs, then the latter effect seems more likely to prevail. The two hypotheses need not be completely discriminating, for instance, we can think of firms of the same size, but located in different countries, that increase their level of sunk costs due to an opening up of new markets.[52] However, this is a somewhat different issue then the question purported in the present paper.

We hence conclude that the endogeniety hypothesis of sunk costs fail to attain support, at least when we extend the analysis to embrace market structures characterized by more then just a few firms, that is, when we leave the "pure"oligopoly world. The level of sunk costs is larger in absolute and relative terms in more sizeable firms. Furthermore, the demising impact of size on firms' endowment of FSA suggest that when we abandon the close world economy and consider the world market, an endogenous relationship between suck costs and market size becomes even less likely.

Notwithstanding that firm growth can be expected to result from both market growth and the strategic decisions taken by a firm, our results indicate that the firm's own explicit decisions to increase its outlays on FSA is a crucial ingredient of growth, rather then a passive adjustment to an increase in market size. Particularly since it seems to enable expansion on foreign markets. Entry on foreign markets, either through exports or by setting up foreign affiliates, also means that the local market structure will be affected.

---

[52] For a life cycle explanation of entry and exits, see Klepper & Graddy (1990) and Jovanovic & McDonald (1994). Mata (1993) conclude that sectors with higher turbulence rates—which could be correlated with size—also have lower sunk cost.

LITERATURE

Acs, Z., Audretsch, D., 1987, "Innovation, Market Structure, and Firm Size", *The Review of Economics and Statistics*, 69, 567-574.

Bain, J., 1949, "A Note on Pricing in Monopoly and Oligopoly", *American Economic Review*, 39, 448-464.

Bain, J., 1955, *Barriers to New Competition*, Harvard University Press: Cambridge.

Brainard, S., 1993, "An Empirical Assessment of the Proximity-Concentration Tradeoff Between Multinational Sales and Trade", *NBER WP*, No. 4269.

Braunerhjelm, P., 1996, "The Relation Between Firm-Specific Intangibles and Exports", *Economic Letters*, 53, 213-19.

Braunerhjelm, P., 1999, "Sunk Costs, Firm Size, and Internationalization", *Weltwirtschaftliches Archiv*, Hefte 4, 1-18.

Cabral, L., 1995, "Sunk Costs, Firm Size and Growth", *The Journal of Industrial Economics*, 63?, 161-172.

Caves, R., 1971, "International Corporations: The Industrial Economics of Foreign Investment", *Economica*, 38, 1-27.

Caves, R., 1996, *Multinational Enterprises and Economic Analysis*, Cambridge University Press: Cambridge.

Cohen, W. & Levin, R., 1989, "Empirical Studies of Innovation and Market Structure", in R. Schmalensee and R. Willig, (eds.), *Handbook of Industrial Organization, Volume II*, North-Holland: Amsterdam.

Cohen, W. & Movery, D., 1987, "Firm Size and R&D Intensity: A Re-examination", *Journal of Industrial Economics*, 35, pp. 543-565.

Dasgupta, P. & Stiglitz, J., 1980, "Industrial Structure and the Nature of Innovative Activity", *Economic Journal*, 90, pp. 266-293.

Dixit, A., "Entry and Exit Decisions Under Uncertainty", *Journal of Political Economy*, 97, 620-638.

Dunne, T., Roberts, M., Samuelson, L., 1989, "The Growth and Failure of US Manufacturing Plants", *Quarterly Journal of Economics*, 104, 671-698.

Dunning, J., 1980, "Toward an Eclectic Theory of International Production: Some Empirical Tests", *Journal of International Business Studies*, 11, pp. 9-31.

Eliasson, G. & Braunerhjelm P., 1998, "Intangible, Human-Embodied Capital and Firm Performance" in Eliasson, G., Green, C. and McCann, C. (eds.), *Microfoundation of Economic Growth*, Michigan University Press, Ann Arbor.

Fors, G., 1997, "Utilization of R&D Results in the Home and Foreign Plants of Multinationals", *Journal of Industrial Economics*, No. 3, 1997. pp.341-358.

Gilbert, R., 1989, "Mobility Barriers and Value of Incumbency", in R, Schmalensee, Willig, R. (eds.), *Handbook of Industrial Organization*, Vol. II, North Holland: Amsterdam.

Greenhalg, C., 1991, "Innovation and Trade Performance in the United Kingdom", *Economic Journal*, 100, pp. 105-118.

Heckman, J., 1976, "The Common Studies of Statistical Models of Truncation, Sample Selection and Limited Dependent Variable and Simple Estimations for Such Models", *Annals of Economic and Social Measurement*, 5, pp. 475-492.

Hirsch, S. & Bijaoui, I, 1985, "R&D and Export Performance: A Micro View", *Weltwirtschaftliches Archiv*, 121, pp. 238-250.

Hughes, K., 1985, "Exports and Innovation. A Simultaneous Model", *European Economic Review*, 30, pp. 383-399.

Hymer, S., 1961, *The International Operations of National Firms: A Study of Direct Foreign Investments*, MIT University Press: Cambridge.

Jovanovic, B., 1982, "Selection and the Evolution of Industry", *Econometrica*, 50, 649-670.

Jovanovic, B., MacDonald, G., 1994, "The Life Cycle of a Competitive Industry", *Journal of Political Economy*, 102, 322-347.

Klepper, S., Graddy, E., 1990, "The Evolution of New Industries and the Determinants of Market Structure", *Rand Journal of Economics*, 2, 27-44.

Kravis, I. & Lipsey, R., 1992, "Sources of Competitiveness of United States and its Multinational Firms", *Review of Economics and Statistics*, 74, pp. 193-201.

Lall, S., 1980, "Monopolistic Advantages and Foreign Investments by U.S. Manufacturing Industry", *Oxford Economic Papers*, 32, pp. 102-122.

Lambson, V., Jensen, F., 1998, "Sunk Costs and Firm Value Variability: Theory and Evidence", *American Economic Review*, 88, 307-313.

Mansfield, E., 1962, "Entry, Gibrat's Law, Innovation, and the Growth of Firms", *American Economic Review*, 52, 1023-1051.

Mata, J., 1993, "The Determinants of Firm Star-up Size", WP 11-93, Banco de Portugal, October.

Mata, J., 1994, "Firm Growth During Infancy", *Small Business Economics*, 6, 27-39.

Ollinger, M., Fernandez & Cornejo, J., 1998, Sunk Costs and Regulation in the U.S. Pesticide Industry, *International Journal of Industrial Organization*, 16, 139-168.

Miesenbock, K, 1989, "Small Business and Exporting: A Literature Review", *International Small Business Journal*, 6, pp. 42-62.

Schmalensee, R., 1986, "Advertising and Market Structure: A Review Article", in J. Stiglitz, Mathewson, G., (eds.), *New Developments in the Analysis of Market Structure*, MIT Press: Cambridge, MA.

Schmalensee, R., 1992, "Sunk Costs and Market Structure: A Review Article", *The Journal of Industrial Economics*, 60, pp. 124-135.

Sutton, J., 1991, *Sunk Costs and Market Structure*, MIT Press: Cambridge.

Svensson, R., 1996, "Effects of Overseas Production on Home Country Exports: Evidence Based on Swedish Multinationals", *Weltwirtschaftliches Archiv*, 132, pp. 304-329.

Swedenborg, B., 1979, *The Multinational Operations of Swedish Firms. An Analysis of Determinants and Effects*, IUI: Stockholm.

Teece, D., 1982, "Towards an Economic Theory of the Multiproduct Firm", *Journal of Economic Behavior and Organization*, 3, pp. 39-63.

Tirole, J, 1994, *The Theory of Industrial Organization*, MIT Press: Cambridge.

White, H.,1980, "A Heteroscedasticity-Consistent Covariance Matrix Estimator and a Direct Test for Heteroscedasticity", *Econometrica*, 48, pp. 817-838.

Williamson, O., 1975, *Market and Hierarchies: Analysis and Antitrust Implications*, Free Press: New York.

APPENDIX TO CHAPTER 4

Two different econometrics techniques will be applied, and we will consider each of them separately.

Sunk Costs and Firm Size

In the first model (Model I), the dependent variable is the firm's level of sunk costs in firm-specific assets (FSA), as defined above, per employee. We focus on the impact of firm size (SIZE) on the level of sunk costs, while controlling for other independent variables, contained in the vector X in equation 4.1,

$$FSA_i = c_i + \alpha_1 SIZE_i + X'_i \alpha_2 + \epsilon_i, \qquad (A4.1)$$

where the subscript i refers to the individual firm. The error term is expected to exhibit standard properties, $\epsilon \sim N(0, \sigma^2)$, and $E(\epsilon_i \epsilon_j) = 0$ for $i \neq j$. The regressions will be undertaken by implementing OLS techniques.

Foreign Entry, Sunk Costs, and Firm Size

The proceeding step in the econometrics analysis (Model II) aims at estimating the impact of sunk costs in firm-specific assets on entry into foreign markets through exports. The dependent variable (EXP/TS) is defined as firm i's export from the home country, divided by total sales. Since the dependent variable contains a large number of zeroes (23 percent), we will implement a censored dependent variable technique in this part of the analysis. If all observations where $(EXP/TS)_i = 0$ were disregarded, then, irrespective of whether the error term in the population has a zero mean and a constant variance, the sample error will not have these properties because observations have been systematically, rather than randomly, excluded. An appropriate statistical technique in this case is the Tobit method (Tobit 1958),

$$\frac{EXP_i^*}{TS_i} = \gamma_0 + \gamma_1 SC^*_i + Z'\gamma_2 + v_i . \qquad (A4.2)$$

$$\frac{EXP_i}{TS_i} = \begin{cases} \dfrac{EXP_i^{\cdot}}{TS_i} & \text{if } \dfrac{EXP_i^{\cdot}}{TS_i} > 0 \\[4mm] 0 & \text{if } \dfrac{EXP_i^{\cdot}}{TS_i} \leq 0 \end{cases} \qquad\qquad (A4.3)$$

Since sunk costs in firm-specific assets—which appeared as the endogenous variable in equation 4.1—is implemented as an explanatory variable with regard to foreign entry through exports, FSA may be correlated with the error term in the Tobit equation (v_i). In that case also ϵ_i and v_i correlated. To take account of this potential source of biasedness, we proceed by estimating Model II as a recursive system. Then the standard properties can be assumed to prevail, i.e., $v \sim N(0, \sigma_v^2)$, $E(v_j v_i) = 0$ for $i \neq j$.

Hence, estimating Model II implies that in the first step OLS-technique is applied and we regress all the exogenous variables in the system on sunk costs in FSA, to obtain a predicted value of sunk costs in firm-specific assets (SC*). Then, in the second step, the actual value of sunk costs in FSA is replaced by the predicted value in the Tobit equations 4.2 and 4.3, which is estimated via maximum likelihood procedures. The implemented control variables are contained in the vector Z. We will also present the results from some additional regressions runs where alternative proxies for sunk costs have been inserted directly into the Tobit function.

Chapter 5

CLUSTERS, VENTURE CAPITAL AND GROWTH

5.1 Introduction

The lack of dynamics and transformation in most European countries stands in stark contrast to economic development in the United States. Forces of renewal within the American economy are reflected in its dominance with respect to new industries (information technology, biotechnology/ biomedicine etc.), diversity of product supply, and an influx of new and growing firms into these industries. In the latter region industrial renewal is more or less exclusively attributed to established firms, while the influx of new, innovative and technology-based firms has been limited during the postwar era.[53]

The question is why no equivalent development has taken place in Europe? Sweden contributes a particularly interesting case among the European countries. For nearly two decades now, Sweden has invested more in R & D in relationship to GDP than any other country. By rights, this should be creating a hotbed of growth for new technology-based firms and leading to significant renewal and dynamics in Swedish industry. Yet, for several decades the Swedish economy has been characterized by low growth, weak expansion of private sector employment and continuing strong dependence on large Swedish corporations compared to other OECD countries.

In previous studies, variables such as lower production costs and greater mobility of production factors—particularly labor—in the U.S. have been proposed as an explanation to these differences (Blanchard and Katz, 1992; Kazamaki Ottersten, 1998). As a result, expanding sectors are not inhibited by a shortage of production factors or prohibitive cost increases. Simultaneously, American academic institutions supply the market with educated labor and pioneering competence, as well as internationally leading research that has constituted the basis for the new knowledge-driven industries.

These factors doubtless contain some truth, but fall short of providing the full explanation. The organization of production must be added to flexibility in a general sense, as well as investments in knowledge. At the corporate level, the organization tends to be more oriented towards the individual employee in the U.S., particularly in knowledge-intensive firms. At the same time, knowledge-intensive production (goods and services) is often concentrated in a well-defined area, both geographically and in the product room. These industry clusters are usually exemplified by Silicon Valley, Hollywood and similar areas. Generally,

---

[53] See Bergman et al. (1999).

cluster environments are characterized by frequent interaction between various players (suppliers, customers, venture capital firms, stale agencies, universities, etc.), a high level of innovation, significant mobility of the labor force, and extensive influx and outflow of companies.[54] The mechanisms behind the cluster dynamic may be summarized as intense competition combined with various complementarities, collaboration and knowledge flows. Accordingly, the dynamics of innovative activities and renewal within the clusters are strongly market driven.

Effective interaction and knowledge transfer between companies demands the presence of certain key players, among them academic institutions and specialized service firms. However, the "bridges" that are perhaps the most important are found in the risk capital market—primarily venture capital firms and "business angels". The existence of these key players is predicated upon a distinct incentive structure which promotes the taking of risks, setting up new establishments, and mobility of firms, capital and labor. In this chapter, we shall study the role played by venture capital firms and corporate angels and, based upon a comparison of Sweden and the Unites States, and highlight the hindrances standing in the way of developing a more effective Swedish venture capital market.

5.2 Industrial Dynamics in Sweden and the United States: A Concise Background

Previous research examining the composition and evolution of similar industry clusters (biomedicine/biotechnology and polymers) in the U.S. have identified significant differences between the regions with respect to industrial dynamics.[55] These differences can to a certain extent be attributed to varying degrees of flexibility in the labor market. The rapid technological transformation and significant investments in real and human capital that characterize new growth industries place great demands on corporate ability to adapt. This has led to changes in the internal organization of companies: flexible work organizations are the guiding principle to ensure that production can be rapidly converted or discontinued. In these organizations, emphasis is placed upon the development of the company's human capital, decentralized areas of responsibility, flat and non-bureaucratic organizations, communication and interaction among the

[54]See Braunerhjelm and Carlsson (1999) for a definition of industry clusters.
[55]For a more detailed description of this research as well as the reasons behind the selection of regions and clusters, see Braunerhjelm and Carlsson, (1996 and 1999); Braunerhjelm, Carlsson and Johansson (1999); Braunerhjelm, Carlsson, Johansson and Karamiouglou, (1998).

employees and an individually-oriented compensation system.[56] Accordingly, contract forms on the American labor market are different and are affected, among other things, by the design of the tax system, e.g., with respect to rules and regulations concerning personal options, profit sharing and other individual incentives.

The most prominent difference between Sweden and the U.S. can however be attributed to the function and structure of the risk capital market, particularly with respect to venture capital. Risk capital in the general sense differs from venture capital in two respects: Venture capital is invested in equity (shares) in unlisted companies, and the venture capitalist is characterized by active involvement in the company in which he invests. However, the explicit purpose of the investment is limited in time, that is, the venture capitalist will exit the company, as a rule after three to seven years, when it is listed or is sold to another stakeholder.

In contrast to the U.S., Sweden has long relied upon state-supplied "venture" capital, while the U.S. has fixed higher credence upon private venture capital firms and other market solutions. Nutek (The Swedish National Board for Industrial and Technical Development) has been the hub of Swedish industrial policy and has had control over the distribution of significant funds earmarked for new businesses, technology and R & D investments.[57] Currently, there are about 140 different kinds of subsidies available to Swedish companies; however, most companies are unaware that they exist and there is no coordination of the various subsidies.

5.3 Venture Capital Firms and "Business Angels"

For many years, the credit market in Sweden was strictly regulated while the banks acted in an oligopolistic market, shielded from outside competition. The big banks often prioritized their major customers where it was considered easier to assess the credit risks of various projects while simultaneously having better insight into the customers' solvency. There was virtually no venture capital available, since opportunities to build private fortunes were sharply limited by the prevailing tax system and savings were mainly administered by the public sector.[58]

---

[56]See e.g., Casey, Shaw and Prennushi (1995), Lee and Reeves (1995), Macduffie (1995) and, for Sweden, Nutek (1996, 1998), and Braunerhjelm (1999).
[57]Total government subsidies to Swedish industry have been estimated at SEK 10 billion for 1995 (Braunerhjelm and Fors, 1998). With respect to seed financing, Nutek, ALMI and Industrifonden (active since 1979), all governmental bodies, have in practice been the dominating players in the Swedish market (see SOU, 1996).
[58]See Black and Gilson (1998) for a comparison of Europe and the U.S. as regards the composition of the risk capital market.

The role of private venture capital is particularly critical within new, knowledge-intensive industries such as biomedicine/biotechnology, where investments are often intangible and future potential difficult to assess (Gompers, 1996). Consequently, considerable specialist ability to assess the market strength of various projects is needed. This applies equally to the company's start-up and growth phases. The tougher competition in the American market has prodded greater diversity and differentiation among venture capital firms and better-educated analysts. In turn, this ha led to a more careful evaluation procedure, which minimizes the problems of adverse selection and moral hazard. This constitutes the basis for more effective distribution of risk capital in the U.S. Nevertheless, American venture capital firms expect no more than a fraction of their investments to be made in truly high-yield projects.

5.3.1 Venture Capital Firms

What does the venture capital firm provide that banks, insurance companies, state institutions and state subsidies and other conceivable financiers, cannot? Apart from providing financial risk capital, it is at least equally important to supply companies with executive competence and market expertise so that new products and research results reach the market. In the U.S., this has long been a self-evident aspect of the venture capital firm's mandate. Several such firms work actively with getting products out to the market. It is precisely this supply of "competent" capital that makes the venture capitalist particularly well-suited to stepping in at a relatively early stage of company development.[59]

Compared to those in many other countries, Swedish venture capital firms invest at relatively late phases and preferably in mature industries (see Figure 5.1). In the U.S., investments are made primarily in new industries, e.g., information technology (IT) and biotechnology, which receive more than 85 percent of venture capital investments. The corresponding figure is 4 percent in Sweden and about 20 percent in the rest of the EU. Table 5.1 illustrates how the investment emphasis in Swedish venture capital firms is directed towards the expansion and maturity phase. Only 3 percent of invested capital can be attributed to the two earliest phases (seed and early growth). This indicates that many of the so-called venture capital firms should rather be classified as investment firms.

The differences between the Swedish and American venture capital markets are founded to a great extent upon the former regulations on the credit markets and the design of the tax system. The earlier deregulation of the American

---

[59]See also Olofsson's (1998) study on technology-based firms, which illustrates the importance of contributions by individuals to the company's earliest development.

Figure 5.2. Distribution of venture capital at different phases of investments in 14 countries 1997, percent of GDP.

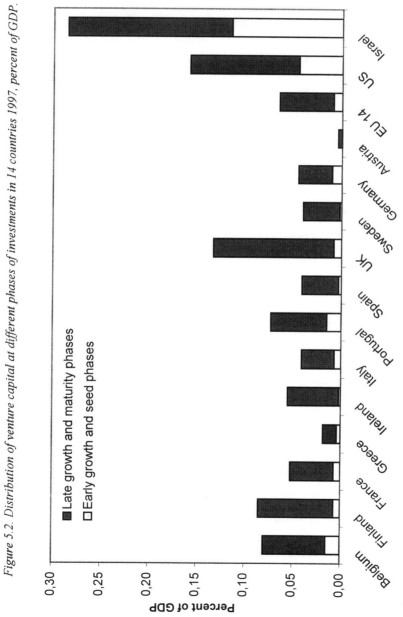

Source: EVCA & KPMG (1998), Bannock Consulting (1998)

Table 5.1. Investments and strategies of Swedish venture capital firms in 1998.

The venture capital firms' main strategy					
	Investment phase				Total
	Seed	Early growth	Expansion	Maturity	
Number of venture capital firms	5	22	22	8	57
Managed capital (SEK millions)	320	3017	18269	24245	45841
Percentage of managed capital in each phase	1	7	40	52	100
Invested capital (SEK millions)	256	1351	4935	7715	13717
Percentage of total managed capital invested in each phase	0.1	2.9	11	17	31
Number of portfolio companies	32	215	286	83	616
Average investment per company (SEK millions)	1.8	6.9	17.3	93	-

Source: Isaksson (1998).

Note: The figures above include all large venture capital firms (both state-owned and private). Since a number of smaller companies may not be included, it is likely that total investments have been somewhat underestimated. For a more detailed description of Swedish venture capital firms, see Isaksson (1998).

market with respect to which players may invest in venture capital funds, has also contributed to greater competition and diversity than is found in the Swedish market. American pension funds were allowed to invest in these funds as early as 1979. American studies show that this strongly influenced the supply of venture capital (Gompers & Lerner, 1998), but the demand for venture capital also rose. This occurred partially because entrepreneurs saw greater opportunities to obtain financing and partially because taxes on capital were lowered drastically during the same period. Compared to those in Europe and Sweden, American institutional investors are also significantly more active in the venture capital market. Even though Swedish institutional investors may place between five and ten percent of their portfolios in unlisted stocks, the percentage is significantly lower in practice.[60] The share invested in unlisted stocks is often as low as 0.1 percent of their capital (Landell et al., 1998). Some change can however be discerned in the Swedish market; for example, it is explicitly stated in the directive to the Sixth Swedish Pension Insurance Fund that the fund shall contribute to the provisioning of risk capital.

The tax system also discriminates against Swedish venture capital firms compared to corporations and investment firms. First, any dividends from the companies in which the venture capital firm invested are taxed, then the venture capital firm's profits are taxed, and finally, the profits distributed to the individuals who have invested in the venture capital firm are taxed.[61] Unlike the usual double taxation of corporate profits (i.e. first profits are taxed, then shareholders pay tax on their dividends), the venture capital firm's profits are triple-taxed.

Income from capital is taxed at a significantly lower rate in the U.S. than in Sweden, provided that the investment was made in a small enterprise and that the stock was retained for a certain period. Furthermore, stimulants to encourage investments in unlisted stocks have been introduced in several countries. In England, for instance, which has the most vital venture capital market in Europe, the Enterprise Investment Scheme (EIS) and the Venture Capital Trust (VCT) system were both launched in the first half of the 1990s. The motive behind these systems is that the investor shall be compensated for the greater risk associated with investments in unlisted companies. EIS is oriented primarily towards direct investments by private individuals, while VCT is composed of listed corporations that mainly invest in unlisted stocks. Both systems are built upon the premise that risk compensation occurs through tax relief. The systems differ somewhat with respect to the format of the tax incentive, but generally speaking, dividends are tax free and capital gains are either tax exempt (if the stock is held for more than five years) or may be deferred if the profits are used for reinvestment in unlisted stocks. The differences in taxation between Sweden and other countries may be expected to lead to more Swedish venture capital firms preferring to be domiciled abroad. There is then a clear and present risk that the focus on Swedish companies will eventually decline, particularly for those in an early phase of their development.

---

[60] The main rule on investments by banks and insurance companies is that they shall be made in listed and liquid stocks. Limitations upon ownership shares in unlisted companies by insurance companies and mutual funds mean that investments tend to be far too small to be interesting for large investors. A proposal has been made to abolish the "five percent rule" for insurance companies, which stipulates that ownership may be no greater than five percent of voting shares.
[61] Through sophisticated company forms (limited partnerships) and enterprises controlled from abroad, it is possible to circumvent some of these regulations. However, maneuvers of this kind are associated with transaction costs in one form or another.

5.3.2 Business Angels and Renewal

Business angels are individuals who have created personal wealth through running their own businesses and then switched over to being financiers and co-investors in new projects (Lerner 1998; Lumme, Mason and Suomi, 1998). In the U.S. first and foremost, these investors have been a vital link in providing opportunities to entrepreneurs to obtain financing. The difference between Sweden and the U.S. is not solely the greater numbers of corporate angels in the latter, but also— and perhaps most importantly—their willingness to provide the companies with risk capital at an early stage, i.e. earlier than most American venture capital firms. It has been estimated that more than half of all corporate angel investments are directed at the seed phase in the U.S., while the corresponding figure in Sweden is about twenty-five percent (Landström, 1993; Bergman 1998).Through their previous experience, business angels possess extensive knowledge in certain lines of industrial production, have extensive contact networks, and considerable know-how in running companies. As a result, they are particularly well-suited to judging the strength and potential of various projects in the very earliest and riskiest phases.

One reason for the richer supply of "angel capital" in the U.S. is the design of the tax system; both income and wealth are taxed at a much higher rate in Sweden. However, it is first and foremost the regulations surrounding closed corporations that impede corporate angels from acting in Sweden. The tax code differentiates between passive —or "sleeping"—and active partners in closed corporations. An individual employed by the company is usually defined as an active partner. Dividend income from holdings of stocks in closed corporations below a given "ceiling amount" are taxed as income from capital, while dividends in excess of that amount are taxed as income from employment.[62] Corporate angels, whose role is precisely to become actively involved, thus risk being taxed in large part as wage earners, i.e., at about 60 percent, as compared to a tax rate of 30 percent on capital income.[63]

When stock is sold, the main rule is that active partners are taxed on 50 percent of profits up to 100 basic amounts (i.e., approximately SEK 3.6 million) as

---

[62] The rules are very detailed and complex. Dividends on stock in unlisted companies are calculated in three steps. In the first step, the so-called tax relief amount, the dividend is tax-free. It is calculated as the government loan interest rate times 0.7 times the capital amount. The capital amount is defined as the acquisition cost of the stock plus the salary total, minus 10 so called "basic amounts", which approximately equals the annual wage cost of one productive worker. Moreover, in order for the salary total to be added to the capital stock, the company must have at least two employees and the active owner's salary must be at least 20 percent higher than that of the employees. The next step, the so-called "ceiling amount", is defined as dividends that equal return on the capital amount up to the government loan interest rate plus five points, which is taxed as income from capital. Dividends over this amount are taxed as income from employment.

[63] It is sufficient that the stockholder is active in the company and has affected its profit.

Table 5.2. Examples of the effects of capital gains taxation upon sale of unlisted stocks by private individuals in 1998 (SEK).

	Investment in unlisted venture capital firms	Investment in listed investment firms	Direct investment in listed corporation	Direct investment in unlisted firms (passive owner)	Direct investment in unlisted firms (active owner)
Taxation at corporate level					
Selling price	5,000	5,000			
Acquisition cost	1000	1000			
Profit	4,000	4,000			
Tax	1,129	56			
Left after tax	2,880	3,944			
Capital gains tax (%)	28	14			
Taxation of the individual					
Selling price	3,880	4,944	5,000	5,000	5,000
Acquisition cost	1,000	1,000	1,000	1,000	1,000
Profit	2,880	3,944	4,000	4,000	4,000
Tax relief	71	0	0	71	71
Portion taxed as income from capital	2,809	3,944	4,000	3,929	2,168
Capital tax 30%	843	1,183	1,200	1,179	650
Portion taxed as income from employment	0	0	0	0	1,761
Income tax 57%	0	0	0	0	1,004
Left after tax	2,037	2,761	2,800	2,821	2,346
Total capital gains tax (%)	**49.1**	**31**	**30**	**29.5**	**41.4**

Source: Ahl & Falck, 1998; Braunerhjelm, 1999.
Note: The conditions for the calculations above are as follows. The investing individual has an income above the threshold, i.e., taxes are 57 percent. The stock is assumed to have been acquired for SEK 1,000 in 1995 and the market value to be SEK 5,000 in 1998. In the corporate cases, the venture capital firm and investment firm first sell their stock, whereupon the private individual sells his stock/interest in these companies. When the calculations were done, consideration was given to the so-called tax relief and ceiling amounts having been saved. Furthermore, the standard taxation of investment firms of 2 percent of the value of the stock is implemented. The cases illustrate various outcomes but are not exact. For example, the tax relief amount depends on how many people are employed by the company in which the private person invests (there are as a rule, few employees in the seed phase). Any wealth taxes, etc., have not been taken into account.

income from employment, while the remaining 50 percent is taxed as income from capital. Capital gains in excess of 100 basic amounts are taxed according to the rules for income from capital. In practice, the regulations mean that the smaller the active partner's investment is, the more heavily he is taxed, since the portion of profits taxed as income from employment is then larger.[64] The effect is that the regulations discriminate against corporate angels.

Table 5.2 summarizes the tax outcome for private individuals for capital gains attributable to investment in a venture capital firm (unlisted stocks) versus an investment company (listed stocks), or a direct investment in an unlisted company (passive or active partner) versus a listed company. In the table the paradoxical effect upon investors who supply both knowledge and capital is illustrated: players in the venture capital market are subjected to significantly heavier taxation than investors who limit themselves to investing capital.

5.4 Concluding Remarks

Dynamic industrial development characterized by knowledge flows, entrepreneurship and product innovations enhances the possibilities of entering a virtuous cycle of growth and increased demand for labor. As discussed above, knowledge is however not enough to create growth. This is well illustrated by Sweden, which invests more in R & D in relation to GDP than any other country in the world, but is nevertheless trailing in terms of growth. Presently, Sweden is ranked 18th in terms of GDP per capita, a dramatic decline from its former ranking among the top five countries in the 1970s and the 1980s. Institutions that promote a flexible labor market, internationally competitive academic and research environments, and well-cultivated links between R & D and the market, are pivotal in this context. The function and structure of the risk capital markets play a particularly important role. Accordingly, if we are to ignite more dynamic development in Sweden, a shift of emphasis must occur towards more market-related solutions that make increased establishment of venture capital firms and active business angels feasible. The current paradox is that individuals who supply companies with both capital and competence are taxed more strenuously than "sleeping" partners.

In order to further reinforce and deepen the European venture capital market, one should consider stimulating this market during a transition period. Some European countries have already introduced such incentives, e.g., limiting capital gains taxes on stock held in unlisted companies (or allowing taxes to be deferred), possibly combined with a risk capital deduction according to the

---

[64]This applies to investments of more than 100 basic amounts (approx. SEK 3.6 million).

English model.[65] Most critical, however, is a deregulation of placement rules for large investors, such as pension funds, and that rules related to closed corporations are modified such that venture capital investors are not discouraged.

Lack of diversity and competition in the venture capital market curbs the dynamics required to begin the process of sustainable growth. A well-functioning risk capital market leads to more "experiments" and lessens the risk that entrepreneurs will be stigmatized if they fail. However, the critical factor is that regulations must not punish active partners or discriminate against investors who venture into future industries where the outcome is, for wholly understandable reasons, uncertain; nor should government programs be allowed to strangle private initiative.

---

[65]As shown by Landell et al. (1998), the investment firm model is not suitable for companies that invest in unlisted stocks.

LITERATURE

Ahl, H & Falck, M, (1998), *Riskkapitalavdraget och andra incitament för investeringar i onoterade företag*, R 1998:38, Nutek, Stockholm.

Bannock Consulting, (1998), "Innovation Finance in Europe. A Pilot Project in Benchmarking", circular, London.

Bergman, F, (1998), "Företagsänglar - en himla stor resurs", circular, Mid-Sweden University.

Bergman, L, Braunerhjelm, P, Fölster, S, Genberg, H & Jakobsson, U, (1999), *Vägen till välstånd*, Center for Business and Policy Studies, Economic Policy Group Report 1999, SNS Förlag, Stockholm.

Blanchard,O. and Katz,O., 1992, "Regional Evolution", *Brookings Papers on Economic Activity*, No. 1, 1-75.

Black, B. and Gilson, R., 1998, "Venture Capital and the Structure of Capital Markets: Bank Versus Stock Markets", *Journal of Financial Economics*, 47, 243-277.

Braunerhjelm, P & Carlsson, B, (1996), "Industriell dynamik - en jämförelse av utvecklingen i Nya Zeeland, Ohio och Sverige", *Ekonomisk Debatt*, 24.

Braunerhjelm, P & Carlsson, B, (1999), "Industry Clusters in Ohio and Sweden 1975-1990," *Small Business Economics*, 12, 279-93.

Braunerhjelm, P, Carlsson, B & Johansson, D (1998), "Industriella kluster, tillväxt och ekonomisk politik", *Ekonomisk Debatt,26*.

Braunerhjelm, P & Fors, G, (1998), "EMU - den nationella industripolitikens återkomst?", in Bernitz, U, Gustafsson, S & Oxelheim, L (editors), *Europaperspektiv 1998*, Nerenius & Santérus förlag, Stockholm.

Braunerhjelm, P, Carlsson, B, Johansson, D & Karaomerliouglu, D, (1998), "The New and the Old: The Evolution of Biomedical and Polymer Clusters", circular.

Casey, I, Shaw, K & Prennushi, G, (1995), "The Effects of Human Resources Management Practices on Productivity", *NBER WP 5333*, NBER.

EVCA & KPMG, (1998), *European Venture Capital Association Yearbook 1998*, Zaventum (www.evca.com) and London.

Gompers, P., 1996, "Grandstanding in the Venture Capital Industry", *Journal of Financial Economics*, 42, 133-156.

Gompers, P & Lerner, J, (1998), "What Drives Venture Capital Fund Raising?", Paper presented at the Brookings Institute Conference, circular.

Isaksson, A, (1998), "En studie av den svenska venture kapitalmarknaden", circular, Umeå University.

Kruzich, J & Fåhraeus, A, (1998), *What Can We Learn From Silicon Valley?* Industrihuset, Stockholm.

Landell, E, Hörnlund, A, Österberg, B, Appelberg, G & Wassgren, S, (1998), *Entreprenörsfonder. Riskkapital till växande småföretag,* Industrilitteratur and Nutek (info 051-1998), Stockholm.

Landström, H, (1993), "Informal Risk Capital in Sweden and Some International Comparisons," *Journal of Business Venturing*, 8, 525-540.

Lee, D & Revees, T, (1995), "Human Resource Strategies and Firm Performance: What Do We Know and Where Do We Need to Go?" *The International Journal of Human Resource Management*, 6.

Lerner, J., 1998, "Angel Financing and Public Policy: An Overview", *Journal of Banking and Finance*, 22, 773-783.

Lumme, A., Mason, C. and Suomi, M., 1998, *Informal Venture Capital*, Kluwer Academic Publishers, Boston, Dordrect, and London.

MacDuffie, J, (1994), "Human Resource Bundles and Manufacturing Performance: Organizational Logic and Flexible Production Systems in the World of Auto Industry," *Industrial and Labor Relations Review*, 48.

OECD, (1996), *Venture Capital and Innovation*, OECD Publications, Paris.

Olofsson, C, (1998), *Teknikbaserade företag i tidig utvecklingsfas*, IMIT, Göteborg and Stockholm.

Ottersten Kazamaki, E, (1998), "Arbetsmarknadsförhållanden - EMU och rigida institutioner," in Bernitz, U, Gustafsson, S & Oxelheim, L (editors), *Europaperspektiv 1999*, Nerenius & Santérus förlag, Stockholm.

Nutek, (1996), Towards Flexible Organizations, B1996:6, Nutek, Stockholm

Nutek, (1998), Flexibilitet skapar produktivitet - Tillverkningsindustrin 1990-95, Nutek, Stockholm.

SOU, (1996), *Kompetens och kapital,* Företagsstödsutredningens betänkande 1996:69, Nordstedts förlag, Stockholm.

Chapter 6

THE INFLUENCE OF AGGLOMERATION ON LARGE FIRMS' INVESTMENTS—EVIDENCE FROM SWEDISH FOREIGN DIRECT INVESTMENT[66]

6.1 Introduction

Since the mid-1980s, foreign direct investment (FDI) has turned into a major force in the global economy, reaching an unprecedented annual growth rate of approximately 25 percent. World FDI flows increased by roughly 35 percent between 1997 and 1998, whereas exports was constant or even declined. FDI is driven by mergers and acquisition, particularly so called cross-border "mega-mergers" which increased by a stunning 74 percent between 1997 and 1998 (UN, 1999). Despite the overwhelming empirical evidence of the increases in firms' foreign operations, it is only in the last decade that locational issues have become a core area in international economics. For a long time the analyses of these issues were strictly confined to economic geographers.

An overall framework to FDI is provided by Dunning's (1977) OLI-approach, relating microeconomic as well as macroeconomic variables to FDI. More rigorous modelling of the location of production based on externalities arising from firms' inability to fully appropriate the return to R&D investments, economies of scale, increased interaction between firms, and localized access to specific skills and capabilities, have been provided by, for instance, Krugman (1991a,b), Venables (1996), Fujita, Krugman and Venables (1999). If such factors gain in importance for firms' competitiveness, they seem to suggest that firms will increasingly concentrate production in geographically well-defined areas, i.e. agglomeration will arise.

The question addressed in this paper concerns how different host country characteristics affect the locational decision of overseas production. Particular attention is paid to the interaction effects of firm- and country-specific characteristics. The main objective is to examine if agglomeration patterns can be detected in Swedish FDI, and to which extent such agglomeration phenomena differs between industries.

As compared to previous studies in this field, the sample selection and methodology are extended. Notably, countries where firms have decided not to establish manufacturing affiliates are included in the sample, not only those where affiliate production actually takes place. We will therefore use estimation

---

[66] A previous and more detailed analysis is presented in Braunerhjelm and Svensson (1996).

techniques that incorporate a censored dependent variable. This makes it possible to distinguish between factors that determine the probability of firms locating production in certain countries, and, on the other hand, how much firms will produce in those countries where affiliates have already been established. In the statistical analysis, a unique data set on Swedish MNCs is combined with country data for most OECD countries as well as the most important Latin American countries.

The chapter is organized as follows. Section 6.2 reviews the theoretical framework of FDI as well as earlier empirical results. The database and sample selection are described in section 6.3. In section 6.4, the econometric methods and the hypotheses are presented. The results are provided in section 6.5, while the final section concludes.

6.2 Foreign Direct Investment and Agglomeration Patterns

6.2.1 Theoretical Background [67]

The theoretical foundation of FDI is still rather fragmented, compiling bits and pieces from different fields of economics to elucidate the locational pattern of firms. The microeconomic foundation of most theories rests on the theory of the firm (Coase, 1937; Williamson, 1975, 1979) and the theory of the firm's internationalization (Hymer, 1960), i.e. transaction costs explanations are invoked. Such microeconomic explanations provide necessary conditions for FDI. They are, however, not sufficient since firms always have the option to substitute FDI for exports from the home country.

The locational literature focuses on why firms in a specific industry tend to be concentrated in certain geographically well-defined areas, even though costs are higher. The rationale for such agglomeration behavior is traditionally ascribed to the advantages arising from (a) demand and supply linkages, and (b) intra-industry technological and information spill-overs, as follows:[68]

Demand and supply linkages. The "new" location theory emphasizes "pecuniary" externalities, defined to be associated with demand and supply linkages, such as the possibility to use joint networks of suppliers and distributions (Krugman, 1991a, b; Fujita, Krugman and Venables, 1999). Economies characterized by high transportation costs, limited manufacturing production and weak economies of scale are shown in these models to have a

---

[67] For a survey on the new economic geography, see Braunerhjelm, Faini, Norman, Ruane and Seabright (2000).
[68] The idea is not new, already Dahmén (1950) stressed the importance of clustering, or in Dahmén's terminology, development blocks, in creating competitive advantages, a tradition pursued at the macro-level by, for instance, Porter (1990).

dispersed manufacturing sector. On the other hand, low transportation costs, coupled with a large manufacturing sector and economies of scale, foster concentration of production.[69] The analysis of the location of firms is normally confined to the pattern *within* countries, although, and more appropriate for our purpose, the same line of reasoning can of course be applied to the location of firms *between* countries. For instance, Venables (1996) shows in a two-country model how low trade costs increase firms' sensitivity to differences in production costs, thereby making them more internationally "footloose". In the case of vertically linked industries, small parametric changes may then result in "catastrophic" effects where extensive relocation of firms leads to an agglomeration of industrial production into one single country.

Spill-overs. Another reason for agglomeration can be derived from the new growth theory (Romer, 1986; Sala-i-Martin, 1990; Englmann and Waltz, 1995; Martin and Ottaviano, 1996). It is argued that knowledge enhancing activities can only partly be appropriated by firms, implying that an externality is created and diffused to other firms, thereby reducing their costs (Vernon, 1960; Griliches, 1979). The spill-over literature is closely linked to earlier research on public goods. Already Henderson (1974) argued that the rent firms derive from public goods – which enter their production functions as unpaid intermediate goods – induces entrance by firms. For regions where such spill-overs are abundant, it would constitute a locational advantage.

A useful framework with regard to FDI is the eclectic approach (Dunning, 1977), i.e. the OLI-theory, which—rather than providing a full theory—discusses the necessary conditions for FDI to take place. The OLI-theory is named after the three main factors influencing FDI: ownership advantages, i.e. firm-specific assets are represented by O, while L stands for country-specific factors, and I refers to the internalization of firms' proprietary assets. The lack of markets for firm-specific assets tends to make transaction costs—or the risk of being exposed to "opportunistic behavior" (Williamson, 1975)—excessively high for arm's length contracts and similar arrangements, which induce internalization of production through FDI. Regarding the locational factors, the OLI-theory maintains that in order to attract FDI the recipient country has to offer some particular country-specific advantage. Such advantages are, for instance, sizable markets, skills or the cost of production factors, and policy-designed incentives. The OLI-theory lacks variables that explain agglomeration tendencies. As mentioned above, R&D spill-overs, linkages to local networks and suppliers as well as the industrial structure and the skill level among employees have been assigned a crucial role in explaining agglomeration. Hence, in order to understand the distribution of production across countries, such local forces related to country- and industry-specific features must be

---

[69] If factor mobility is low, such agglomeration could be halted by increases in factor rewards.

included in the empirical model.

6.2.2 Previous Empirical Results

To what extent have agglomeration effects been confirmed in empirical research? Most empirical analyses test the impact of country-specific location factors on the flows of FDI (i.e. factors belonging to the L in the OLI-framework). For instance, Swedenborg (1979, 1982) suggests that the market size is one of the most important host country determinant of overseas production. Kravis and Lipsey (1982) and Veugelers (1991) conclude that size and geographical proximity exert a positive impact on the distribution of investments. With regard to openness, broadly defined as access to other countries' markets, evidence is more scattered. Kravis and Lipsey (1982) and Culem (1988) find that it has a positive influence on FDI, giving tentative support to the new locational theory, while Wheeler and Mody (1992) and Brainard (1993b) report opposite results and Veugelers (1991) fails to detect any significant impact. Factor costs seem to have very limited influence on FDI, at least among industrialized countries. In fact, Kravis and Lipsey (1982) report a pattern of "opposite attracts", i.e. firms in low wage industries invested in high-wage markets, where high wages were interpreted as reflecting high productivity. Swedenborg (1979, 1982) reports that high wages in the host country attract MNCs and Brainard (1993a) concludes that factor costs have no impact on the locational decision of FDI.[70] Braunerhjelm (1994) and Braunerhjelm el al (2000), find strong support for a negative impact of high relative production costs on the location of firms.

Thus, from the studies cited above a number of variables can be distinguished that influence the locational choice of firms, although less light is shed on the tendencies towards agglomeration. One exception is the study by Wheeler and Mody (1992) where country characteristics, such as the quality of infrastructure, the degree of industrialization and the level of inward FDI into the respective market, are incorporated into the analysis as measures of agglomeration factors. It is contended that US investors regard such agglomeration factors as one of the major determinants of FDI. Wheeler and Moody also raise the question how economies that lack such attracting factors can overcome this drawback, since agglomeration—after a certain stage has been reached—seems to be a self-perpetuating process. As shown by Arthur (1986), a minor regional advantage could turn into a substantial clustering of a specialized industrial activity. Some further evidence of agglomeration is also found in the pattern of Japanese FDIs

---

[70] The effects of disparate tax systems are frequently neglected in these studies. Location is, however, not immune to tax differences, although recent integration of markets has induced more of tax-neutrality, particularly with regard to corporate taxes (Modén, 1993).

(Micossi and Viesti, 1991). Japanese firms have predominantly entered into industries in which the host countries have already revealed comparative advantages. Also Head, Ries and Swenson (1995) find support for agglomeration, analyzing Japanese firms in the U.S. Other studies report less unambiguous results. Ellison and Glaeser (1997) conclude that no distinct pattern of concentration can be detected in U.S. location of production. Hanson (1998) and Amiti (1997, 1998) report findings pointing in the opposite direction.

6.3 The Database and Sample Selection

The data set on Swedish MNCs has been collected by the Industrial Institute for Economic and Social Research (IUI) in Stockholm at seven different occasions since the mid-1960s. It contains detailed information about production, employment, R&D and the distribution between foreign and domestic units, as well as the extent and direction of external and internal trade flows. The empirical analysis comprise the period 1978–1990 are used since the emphasis is on the location undertaken by Swedish MNCs in the 1980s. Only countries for which we have export statistics of the individual firms are included in the analysis, i.e. the OECD countries in Europe and North America, and the major countries in Latin America.[71] This is, however, not a cause of great concern since more than 95 percent of the foreign production of Swedish MNCs is undertaken in these countries. Data on country and industry level, if not specified elsewhere, are taken from UN (1980, 1989, 1993) statistics.

In studying how different factors affect the pattern of foreign production, we introduce a methodological novelty. The model is based on the fact that the firm has to make two decisions simultaneously when locating overseas production: (1) Whether to establish a manufacturing affiliate in a country at all; (2) If an affiliate is established, what level of operation should then be chosen? The alternative to choosing a high level of production in a country may, in fact, be to locate no production there at all, rather than choosing a low level of production. Furthermore, the firm can always exit the market even if sunk costs are present, e.g. by selling or closing down the affiliate.

Previous studies have only considered countries where affiliate production actually takes place, which means that the first decision has been ignored. Since the two decisions are interrelated, systematic sample selection bias will be present and the parameter estimates will be both biased and inconsistent. We avoid this problem by including in our sample also countries where the firm has not established any manufacturing affiliates.

---

[71] EC countries: Germany, the Netherlands, Belgium, France, Italy, United Kingdom, Denmark, Spain and Portugal; EFTA countries: Norway, Finland, Switzerland and Austria; North America: the United States and Canada; Latin America: Argentina, Brazil and Mexico.

One could imagine countries where a certain firm would never invest. In particular lack of knowledge or experience of a country would deter investments. Table 6.1 shows the connection between the establishment of manufacturing affiliates abroad and the previous trade pattern of Swedish MNCs over the 1975-90 period. As many as 94 percent of all entries were located in markets to which the firms had previously exported. We could interpret this as if a certain amount of knowledge had been acquired through the firms' exports to the market. Countries to which firms export should therefore be strong candidates for FDI.[72] Exceptions to this pattern relate to industries where serious trade barriers have made export impossible, as in the gas (chemicals), concrete, food and textile (others) industries.

Table 6.1. Comparison between establishment of affiliates and firms' earlier exports, by industry, 1975-1990.

Industry	No. of estab-lishments	No. of obs. to which the firms had previous exports	Percent
Paper & pulp	44	43	99
Chemicals	73	62	85
Iron & steel	15	15	100
Metal products	35	31	89
Machinery	77	76	99
Electronics	108	107	99
Transports	16	16	100
Others [a]	50	42	84
All industries	418	392	94

Note: Every time a firm has established an affiliate in a host country, one observation is generated. Only firms which are included in two succeeding surveys are analyzed in the table, i.e. observations for 1990 (1986, 1978) are only included when a firm appears in the 1986 (1978, 1974) survey as well.
[a] 'Other' industries include the food, textile, paper products, wood products and concrete industries.

In the empirical analysis one observation is generated every time the firm has had previous export to a foreign market, irrespective of whether the firm has established any affiliates in the particular country. According to the sample criteria, a firm in the 1990 (1986, 1978) survey is only included in the sample when it appears in the 1986 (1978, 1974) survey as well.

---

[72] It should be noted that affiliates are not established in all markets where the firm has previously exported.

6.4 Hypotheses for Empirical Testing

The explanatory variables included in the model are primarily derived from the OLI-framework, extended to incorporate country-specific agglomeration factors. The focus will be on the interaction between firm- and country-specific determinants of FDI. All variables except those measuring agglomeration and the previous trade pattern of the investing firm have been used in earlier studies.

Agglomeration. In line with the discussion in section II, a variable measuring country agglomeration effects ($AGGL_{bjt}$) is introduced. It is defined as the share of employees in industry b – in which the investing firm operates – of all employees in the manufacturing sector in host country j at time t.[73] For two reasons, this variable is divided with a weighted mean of the share of employees in industry b in all countries: First, some industries may be large in almost all countries and, second, some industries are more labor intensive than others. Such industries would then receive a lower value if we had chosen the share of output instead.

In our view, this variable should capture local support systems and networks within industries, but it could also be interpreted as a proxy for possible intra-industry R&D spill-overs. Thus, if the coefficient of $AGGL$ turns out to be significantly positive, it suggests a presence of agglomeration effects.[74] Insignificant or negative parameter estimates imply that firms primarily invest in countries which have limited production of similar products, indicating that other reasons to invest abroad are more important. This specification of the agglomeration variable allows a more disaggregated analysis as compared to the approach taken by Wheeler and Mody (1992) and Micossi and Viesti (1991). It is more along the lines of Head, Ries and Swenson (1996). See also Braunerhjelm et al (1999).[75]

Additional host country characteristics. The other country variables included in the model are as follows. Large markets, measured by GDP, are

---

[73] Industry b for the agglomeration variable refers to the 3-digit ISIC-level for engineering and 2-digit level for other industries. It is difficult to collect country data on a finer industry level, although the industry classification for the Swedish MNCs can be obtained on an extremely fine level. It would be preferable to have industry data on a regional level in each country, but information on the regional location of the Swedish-owned foreign affiliates were not available.

[74] One may argue that there should be a simultaneous relationship between NS/TS and $AGGL$, e.g. if firms in electronics allocate more FDIs to Germany, then this industry will get a larger share of total manufacturing employees in Germany. This is, however, not a problem of great concern, since our model analyzes location of affiliate production for individual firms. It is quite farfetched to believe that an individual firm would affect a characteristic aggregated on industry and country level.

[75] It could be argued that $AGGL$ partly measures comparative advantages, e.g. supply of skilled labor or large demand of the firm's products in the host country. By including other host country variables, however, we will control for such factors.

supposed to capture demand and scale effects. GDP_{jt} has received support in most empirical analyses, and is expected to have a positive influence on host country production. Moreover, a variable measuring the relative endowment of skilled labor in the host country is included. This is defined as the number of research scientists, engineers and technicians per 1000 of the population ($RSET_{jt}$). Host countries with high $RSET$ values are expected to promote FDI, especially by R&D intensive firms.

A modified version of the Wheeler and Mody (1992) index measuring openness of the host country has also been included ($OPEN_{jt}$).[76] $OPEN$ takes on values from 1 to 10, where 10 means high openness. Here we assume that protection encourages MNCs to locate production in the host country. Another index measures the physical distance between Sweden and the host country ($DIST_{jt}$). It is assumed that $DIST$ captures "how difficult it is to do business with a particular country" from the Swedish point of view (Nordström, 1991). The higher the value of $DIST$, the lower the probability, as well as the intensity, to produce in the country.[77]

According to the discussion in section 6.3, establishment of production should be facilitated if the firm already has some information about the host country, since knowledge tends to reduce the risk associated with foreign investment. The historical trade pattern of the firm indicates whether such knowledge has been acquired. Here, it is represented by the parent exports of finished goods by firm i to country j in period $t-1$ ($XF_{ij,t-1}$). To control for scale factors on firm level and historical factors, XF_{t-1} is weighted with the inverse of the firm's total sales in period $t-1$. By using the lagged value of exports, we make an attempt to avoid simultaneity problems.[78] Large exports at an earlier stage are expected to have a positive influence on the location of production (Aharoni, 1966; Johansson and Vahlne, 1977).

Firm characteristics. Some firm characteristics are included as control variables. In accordance with the OLI-theory, ownership advantages are

---

[76] This index includes (1), limits to foreign ownership and, (2), government requirements that a certain percentage of a specific type of local components must be used in production. The Wheeler-Mody index was constructed for the US and it has been modified to conform better with the Swedish situation by including the data on trade barriers in Leamer (1990).

[77] This variable takes both (1), geographical and, (2), cultural and linguistic distance into account. The former should favor production relative to exports to avoid costs of shipping over long distances, while the latter should exert a negative impact on both exports and production according to the transactional approach. In practice, this means the following ranking: Nordic countries, other North European countries, North America, South European countries, and, finally, Latin America.

[78] In Svensson (1993), it is discussed and shown how foreign production and exports are simultaneously related to each other.

expected to create absolute advantages vis-à-vis competitors.[79] We use R&D intensity (RD_{it})—defined as total R&D expenditures divided by total sales of the firm—and the average wage (LS_{it}) in the home country part of the MNC, to capture such advantages. The former is argued to capture the technological intensity of the firm, while the latter should be correlated with the human capital within the company. Both RD and LS should exert a positive impact on the propensity to produce abroad.

Another firm-specific variable, high initial capital costs (HIC_{it}), limits competition since it makes it costly for new firms to enter the market. HIC therefore renders a competitive advantage for firms already in the market and is expected to exert a positive impact on overseas production. HIC is the average plant size, measured as the average book value of real estate, equipment and tools, of the MNC's foreign affiliates.[80]

Dummies. By including additive dummy variables, we examine whether any shifts in the level of the dependent variable occur over time or across regions.[81] The analysis also considers whether there are any industry- or firm-specific fixed effects to explain the variation in foreign production. This is done by assigning additive dummies for different industries in model (I) and firms in model (II).[82]

In models (I) and (II), all parameters to the explanatory variables are restricted, i.e. they are assumed to have the same value for all industries. In an additional run of model (II), however, the parameter of $AGGL$ is allowed to vary across high and low technology industries.[83] This is accomplished by assigning an interaction dummy to $AGGL$ for one of the industry groups.

---

[79] It is expected that such advantages should, in the first place, affect the overall presence on foreign markets (probit equation) and not the distribution of production across countries (OLS equation).

[80] This definition is made under the assumption that each affiliate operates at the optimal level of scale.

[81] The regions are the EC, EFTA, North America (Nam) and Latin America (Lam).

[82] The industry dummies are assigned on the 4-digit ISIC-level for engineering and 3-digit level for other industries. The treatment of engineering is motivated by the fact that a majority of the firms belongs to this industry. When controlling for firm-specific effects, MNCs included in at least two of the three surveys are given an additive dummy. This means that we control for 27 different firms, which cover more than 75 percent of the observations. There is no use to assign dummies to MNCs which only appear in one survey, since there is little variation left between firms.

[83] The group of high-technology industries are pharmaceuticals, plastic and rubber products, and the entire engineering industry. The low-technology group includes food, textiles, wood products, paper & pulp, iron & steel and basic chemicals.

6.5 Results of the Estimations

Two empirical methods, described in the appendix, will be implemented in the analysis. The results of the first method (Tobit estimations) are shown in Table 6.2. The parameter to the agglomeration variable, *AGGL*, is positive and at least significant on the 10-percent level. The more important the industry of the investing firm is in the host country, the more the firm's affiliate will produce in that country, and the higher the probability that the firm has established any affiliate there. This result gives some support to the view that agglomeration forces partly determines the location of manufacturing affiliates. It is, however, even more clearly confirmed that the previous trade pattern of the firm affects the location of production. The parameter to the export variable, *XF/TS*, is significant at the 1-percent level in both runs.

Both market size, *GDP*, and the endowment of skilled labor, *RSET*, exert a positive and clearly significant impact on affiliate production. This is in accordance with the hypotheses above. The openness of the host country, *OPEN*, has the expected negative impact on affiliate production, but the parameter is never significant. It is also shown that the physical distance between Sweden and the host country matters. The parameter of *DIST* has an expected negative sign and is significant at the 5-percent level in both models.

Turning to the firm-specific control variables, the R&D intensity, *RD*, labor skill, *LS*, as well as scale economies on plant level, *HIC*, have the expected positive connection to foreign production, but the parameters are not always significant. Not surprisingly, the coefficients of the firm variables are strongly affected by the inclusion of firm-specific effects in model (II). The impact of *RD* is then significant, while the influences of *LS* and *HIC* are no longer significant.

Table 6.3 shows the results of the second method (SBCR estimations), where the probability and marginal effects are separated. *AGGL* exerts a clearly significant impact on the probability that the firm locates affiliates in the host country, while the marginal effect is only significant in model (II). Taken together, this suggests that agglomeration effects are present in FDI. The parameters of *XF/TS*, *GDP* and *RSET* are all positive and, with one exception, significant at the 5-percent level in both the probit and the OLS equations in models (I) and (II). In contrast to the results reported in Table 6.2, *OPEN* now turns out to have a significant impact on the level of production in the affiliates in the OLS equation, while it has no influence on the dichotomous location decision in the probit equation. The parameter of *DIST* has the expected negative sign, but the significance is stronger in the probit equation. Once again, the coefficients of the firm control variables change their magnitude and significance when comparing models (I) and (II), especially for *LS* and *HIC*. The p-value varies substantially between the probit and OLS equations.

Almost all variables except *OPEN* exert a significant impact on the dichotomous location decision in the probit equation. On the other hand, the parameters of all host country characteristics, except *AGGL* and *DIST*, are strongly significant in the OLS equation, while the results for the firm variables are weak as expected.

Table 6.2. Estimation results of the Tobit method (equation 6.1).

Method = Tobit	Dependent variable = *NS/TS*	
Independent variables	Model (I)	Model (II)
AGGL	1.207 ** (0.480)	0.871 * (0.463)
$(XF/TS)_{t-1}$	21.04 *** (7.44)	32.94 *** (8.01)
GDP	9.94 E-5 ** (4.31 E-5)	1.05 E-4 ** (4.22 E-4)
RSET	0.321 ** (0.157)	0.329 ** (0.157)
OPEN	-0.224 (0.233)	-0.217 (0.232)
DIST	-0.067 *** (0.024)	-0.068 *** (0.023)
RD	22.88 (15.21)	47.82 *** (14.95)
LS	0.021 *** (7.09 E-3)	5.65 E-3 (8.02 E-3)
HIC	7.77 E-3 *** (2.66 E-3)	4.56 E-3 (3.92 E-3)
Log likelihood ratio	1068	1187
No. of observations	1330	1330
Left censored obs.	769	769

Note: Standard errors in parentheses. ***, ** and * indicate significance at 1, 5 and 10 percent respectively. Intercept and dummies for time, regions and industries are not shown, but available on request.

Table 6.3. Estimation results of the SBCR method (equations 6. 2-6.4).

Method = SBCR	Probit	OLS	Probit	OLS
Dependent variable	Y	NS/TS	Y	NS/TS
Independent variables	Model (I)		Model (II)	
AGGL	0.261 ** (0.111)	8.62 E-3 (0.013)	0.242 ** (0.114)	0.020 *** (7.72 E-3)
$(XF/TS)_{t-1}$	3.816 ** (1.624)	0.499 * (0.257)	6.674 *** (1.737)	0.597 ** (0.233)
GDP	2.72 E-5 *** (9.98 E-6)	4.12 E-6 *** (9.71 E-7)	2.73 E-5 *** (1.02 E-5)	4.00 E-6 *** (7.49 E-7)
RSET	0.084 ** (0.038)	9.64 E-3 *** (3.45 E-3)	0.097 ** (0.039)	8.03 E-3 *** (2.75 E-3)
OPEN	-0.059 (0.054)	-9.50 E-3 *** (3.05 E-3)	-0.057 (0.056)	-0.011 *** (2.73 E-3)
DIST	-0.014 *** (5.31 E-3)	-1.03 E-3 * (5.30 E-4)	-0.015 *** (5.48 E-3)	-1.13 E-3 ** (4.47 E-4)
RD	9.509 *** (3.344)	0.233 (0.421)	14.81 *** (3.46)	0.082 (0.396)
LS	6.47 E-3 *** (1.55 E-3)	8.11 E-5 (2.75 E-4)	3.20 E-3 * (1.84 E-3)	-3.44 E-4 * (1.89 E-4)
HIC	1.89 E-3 *** (5.97 E-4)	1.52 E-4 * (9.56 E-5)	8.46 E-4 (9.27 E-4)	-4.08 E-5 (6.72 E-5)
λ	---	0.079 (0.053)	---	0.086 ** (0.037)
F-value	---	7.48	---	8.80
Adjusted R^2	---	0.29	---	0.37
No. of observations	1330	561	1330	561
No. of $Y=0$	769	---	769	---
No. of wrong predictions (percent)[a]	28.5	---	25.6	---

Note: Standard errors in parentheses. ***, ** and * indicate significance at 1, 5 and 10 percent respectively. Intercepts and dummies for time, regions and industries in model (I) are not shown, but available on request.

Table 6.4. Testing the impact of AGGL across industry groups.

Method = SBCR		Probit	OLS	Probit	OLS
Dependent variable		Y	NS/TS	Y	NS/TS
Industries		Model (I)		Model (II)	
AGGL	High-tech	0.361 *** (0.135)	0.015 (0.016)	0.267 ** (0.127)	0.022 ** (0.010)
	Low-tech	0.151 (0.139)	2.93 E-3 (0.012)	0.211 (0.134)	0.018 ** (8.76 E-3)

Note: Standard errors in parentheses. ***, ** and * indicate significance at 1, 5 and 10 percent respectively. Complete estimations of the parameters to the explanatory variables are shown not shown, but available on request.

When we allow the parameter of *AGGL* to vary across industry groups in Table 6.4, *AGGL* has a positive, and significant, influence on the dichotomous location decision in high-tech industries, but not in low-tech industries. In the OLS equations, the coefficient of *AGGL* is not significant in any of the industry groups in model (I), which can be compared with the main estimation in Table 6.3. In model (II), the parameter is significant on the 5-percent level for both groups. Furthermore, the difference in the parameter of *AGGL* between the groups is never significant in any of the four runs. On the whole, however, it suggests that agglomeration effects are somewhat more prevalent in high-tech industries.

6.6 Concluding Remarks

The statistical analysis shows that overseas operations by Swedish firms are positively affected by host countries having large production in the same industry that the investing firm belongs to. Such agglomeration influences are strongest in technologically more advanced industries. Hence, the role allotted in contemporary research to supply and demand linkages, as well as knowledge spillovers, receives support in the statistical analysis. However, other forces related to comparative advantages and intra-industry specialization may also show up as agglomeration.

Yet, the remaining host country variables, except for openness, all exert a stronger impact on the localization of production. This is particularly obvious with regard to the previous trade pattern of the firm, as well as the market size and labor skill in host countries.

The sample selection and methodology were extended compared to previous studies. The sample also included countries where the firm had no production, which means that estimation techniques that incorporate a censored dependent variable have been used. This allowed us to analyze separately the two decisions that firms have to take as they consider overseas production; First, whether to locate production in certain host countries at all, and, second, how much to produce if affiliates are established. The statistical analysis show that these two decisions are partly determined by different factors.

If economies of agglomeration turn out to be increasingly important in firms' investment decisions, then according to the new growth theory, this could have repercussions on the rate of growth across countries. Multiple equilibrium situations are possible, where countries, or regions, are trapped in either virtuous or vicious growth cycles. Although the results of the above analysis are based on the investment patterns of Swedish MNCs, we believe they have a general application to MNCs of other countries.

LITERATURE

Aharoni, Y., 1966, *The Foreign Investment Process*, Division of Research, Graduate School of Business Research, Harvard University.

Amiti, M., 1997, "Inter-Industry Trade in Manufacturing. Does Country Size Matter?", *Journal of International Economics*, 44.

Amiti, M., 1998, "New Trade Theories and Industrial Location in the EU: A Survey of Evidence", *Oxford Review of Economic Policy*, 14, 45-53.

Arthur, B., 1986, Industry Location Pattern and the Importance of History, CEPR Paper No. 84, Stanford University.

Brainard, S.L., 1993a, An Empirical Assessment of the Factor Proportions Exploration of Multinational Sales, NBER WP No. 4583.

Brainard, S.L., 1993b, An Empirical Assessment of the Proximity/Concentration Trade-Off between Multinational Sales and Trade, NBER WP No. 4580.

Braunerhjelm, P., 1994, Regional Integration and the Location of Multinational Corporations, IUI, Stockholm.

Braunerhjelm, P., Faini, R., Norman, V., Ruane, F. and Seabright, P., 2000, *Towards a New Geography in Europe*, Monetary European Integration 10, CEPR, London.

Coase, R., 1937, The Nature of the Firm, *Economica,* 4, pp. 13-16.

Culem, C., 1988, The Locational Determinants of Direct Investment Among Industrialized Countries, *European Economic Review*, 32, pp. 885-904.

Dahmén, E., 1950, *Svensk industriell företagarverksamhet*. IUI, Stockholm.

Dunning, J., 1977, Trade, Location of Economic Activities and the MNE: A Search for an Eclectic Approach, in *The Allocation of International Production*, Ohlin, B., Hesselborn, P-O., and Wijkman, P-M. (eds.), Proceedings of a Nobel Symposium in Stockholm, MacMillan, London.

Ellison, G. and Glaeser, E., 1997, "Geographic Concentration in U.S. Manufacturing Industries. A Dartboard Approach", *Journal of Political Economy*, 105, pp. 889-927.

Englmann, F. and Walz, U., 1995, Industrial Centers and Regional Growth in the Presence of Local Inputs, *Journal of Regional Science*, 35, 3-27.

Formby, T.B., Hill, R.C., and Johnson, S.R., 1986, *Advanced Econometric Methods*, Springer-Verlag, New York.

Fujita, M, Krugman P., and Venables, A., 1999, The Spatial Economy, MIT Press, Cambridge, Ma.

Griliches, Z., 1979, Issues in Assessing the Contribution of Research and Development to Productivity Growth, *Bell Journal of Economics*, 10, pp. 92-116.

Hanson, G., 1998, North American Economic Integration and Industry Location, *Oxford Review of Economic Policy,* 14, 30-43..

Head, K., Ries, J. and Swensson, D., 1995, "Agglomeration Benefits and Locational Choice: Evidence From Japanese Manufacturing Investments in the

United States", *Journal of International Economics*, 10, 92-116.

Henderson, J., 1974, A Note on Economics of Public Intermediate Goods, *Economica*, 41, pp. 322-327.

Hymer, S., 1960, *The International Operations of National Firms: A Study of Direct Foreign Investments*, MIT Press, Cambridge, Ma.

Johansson, J. and J.E. Vahlne, 1977, The Internationalization Process of the Firm: A Model of Knowledge Development and Increasing Foreign Direct Commitments, *Journal of International Business Studies*, 8, pp. 23-32.

Kravis, I. and R.E. Lipsey, 1982, The Location of Overseas Production and Production for Export by US Multinational Firms, *Journal of International Economics*, 12, pp. 201-223.

Krugman, P., 1991a, Increasing Returns and Economic Geography, *Journal of Political Economy*, 99, pp. 483-500.

Krugman, P., 1991b, *Geography and Trade*, MIT Press, Cambridge, Ma.

Leamer, E., 1990, The Structure and Effects of Tariffs and Nontariff Barriers in 1983, in *The Political Economy of International Trade*, Jones, R., and Krueger, A. (eds.), Basil Blackwell, Oxford.

Martin, P. and Ottaviano, G, 1996,.Growth and Agglomeration, CEPR Papers No. 1529, CEPR, London.

McDonald, J.F. and R.A. Moffitt, 1980, The Uses of Tobit Analysis, *The Review of Economics and Statistics*, 62, pp. 318-321.

Micossi, S. and G. Viesti, 1991, Japanese Direct Manufacturing Investment in Europe, in *European Integration: Trade and Structure*, Winters, A., and Venables, A. (eds.), Cambridge University Press, New York.

Modén, K.M., 1993, *Tax Incentives of Corporate Mergers and Foreign Direct Investments*, dissertation, The Industrial Institute for Economic and Social Research, Stockholm.

Nordström, K.A., 1991, *The Internationalization Process of the Firm - Searching for New Patterns and Explanations*, Stockholm School of Economics, Stockholm.

Porter, M., 1990, *The Competitive Advantage of Nations*, The Free Press, New York.

Romer, P., 1986, Increasing Returns to Scale and Long-Run Growth, *Journal of Political Economy*, 94, pp. 1002-1037.

Sala-i-Martin, X., 1990, Lecture Notes on Economic Growth, NBER WP No. 3563 and 3564, Cambridge, Ma.

Swedenborg, B., 1979, *The Multinational Operations of Swedish Firms. An Analysis of Determinants and Effects*, IUI, Stockholm.

Swedenborg, B., 1982, *Svensk industri i utlandet. En analys av drivkrafter och effekter (Swedish industry abroad. An analysis of driving-forces and effects)*, IUI, Stockholm.

Svensson, R., 1993, Production in Foreign Affiliates: Effects on Home Country Exports and Modes of Entry, Licentiate thesis, IUI, Stockholm.

Tobin, J., 1958, Estimations of Relationships for Limited Dependent Variables, *Econometrica,* 26, pp. 24-36.

United Nations, 1992, *Statistical Yearbook 1988/89*, 37, United Nations, New York.

United Nations, 1994, *World Investment Report*, United Nations, New York.

Venables, A., 1993, Equilibrium Locations of Vertically Linked Industries, CEPR Discussion Paper 82, London School of Economics, London.

Veugelers, R., 1991, Locational Determinants and Ranking of Host Countries: An Empirical Assessment, *Kyklos,* 44, pp. 363-382.

Wheeler, D. and A. Mody, 1992, International Investment Locational Decisions - The Case of U.S. Firms, *Journal of International Economics,* 33, pp. 57-76.

White, H., 1980, A Heteroscedasticity-Consistent Covariance Matrix Estimator and a Direct Test for Heteroscedasticity, *Econometrica*, 48, pp. 817-838.

Williamson, O., 1975, *Market and Hierarchies: Analysis and Antitrust Implications*, The Free Press, New York.

Williamson, O., 1979, Transaction Costs Economics: Origin, Evolution, Attributes, *Journal of Economic Literature*, 19, pp. 1537-1568.

APPENDIX TO CHAPTER 6

Econometric Methods

The dependent variable is net sales of firm $i's$ affiliates located in country j at time t, NS_{ijt}.[84] NS is divided with total sales of the firm, TS_{it}, in order to control for historical factors as well as economies to scale on the firm level. This is also a way to avoid heteroscedasticity. The variable NS/TS is characterized by a large share of zeroes (more than 60%), since countries where firms have no affiliate production are included as well as countries where affiliates are established. Under these circumstances, one appropriate statistical method for estimating the variation in overseas production is the Tobit method via maximum likelihood procedures (Tobin, 1958):

$$\frac{NS_{ijt}^{*}}{TS_{it}} = \beta_0 + Z'\beta_1 + \epsilon_{ijt} , \qquad (A6.1a)$$

$$\frac{NS_{ijt}}{TS_{it}} = \begin{cases} \dfrac{NS_{ijt}^{*}}{TS_{it}} & if \quad \dfrac{NS_{ijt}^{*}}{TS_{it}} > 0 \\[3mm] 0 & if \quad \dfrac{NS_{ijt}^{*}}{TS_{it}} \leq 0 \end{cases} \qquad (A6.1b)$$

Z is a vector of attributes related to either the MNC or the host country, while β_1 denotes the vector of parameters showing the impact of the Z's on NS/TS. The latent variable $(NS/TS)^{*}$ can be interpreted as an index of the propensity to produce in a specific host country. The residuals are assumed to have the properties $\epsilon \sim (0, \sigma_{\epsilon}^{2})$, $E(\epsilon_{hjt}\epsilon_{ijt})=0$ for $h \neq i$ and $E(\epsilon_{ijt}\epsilon_{ikt})=0$ for $j \neq k$. It should be noted that $E(\epsilon_{ijs}\epsilon_{ijt}) \neq 0$ for $s \neq t$, since a firm which has a high production in country j at time s, is also expected to have a high production at time t. This will, however, not yield inconsistent parameter estimates.[85]

---

[84] Net sales = Gross sales - Imports from the parent company.

[85] The efficiency of the parameter estimates will be reduced by this possible auto-correlation. In the model, we use unbalanced panel data for three time periods, i.e. it is far from always that a combination of a specific firm and country is included the maximum number of three times in the sample. This will partly reduce the auto-correlation problem. To further reduce the auto-correlation we could specify fixed effects for each combination of firm and country in the form of additive dummies, but we would then suffer from a large loss of degrees of freedom and the

If only countries where affiliate production actually takes place are considered and observations are omitted for which $NS/TS=0$, this is equivalent to omitting all observations for which $\epsilon_{ijt} \leq -(\beta_0+Z'\beta_j)$. This implies that if ϵ_{ijt} in the population has a zero mean and a constant variance, the sample error μ_{ijt} will not have these properties because observations have been systematically rather than randomly excluded.

The estimates of the Tobit parameters reflect both changes in the probability of being above the limit and changes in the value of the dependent variable if it is already above the limit. The decomposition is shown in McDonald and Moffitt (1980), but the problem is that the two separate effects will always have the same sign and significance. There may be cases where the probability and marginal effects of a certain explanatory variable differ. It is, however, possible to estimate these impacts separately by using a selection bias corrected regression method, SBCR (Formby et al., 1986). First, a probit function is estimated via maximum likelihood procedures for all observations, both $NS/TS>0$ and $NS/TS=0$, in order to obtain the probability effects:

$$F^{-1}(Pr(Y)_{ijt}) = J_{ijt} = \alpha_0 + Z'\alpha_1 , \qquad (A6.2)$$

where F^{-1} is the inverse of the cumulative standard normal distribution and Y takes the value of one if $NS/TS>0$, and zero if $NS/TS=0$. $Pr(Y)_{ijt}$ represents the probability that firm i has production in country j at time t, given the values of the explanatory variables. The α's are parameters that show the influence of the independent variables on the probability that the firm locates production in a certain country. From these estimates, a sample selection correction variable λ, called Heckman's lambda, is computed for all observations:

$$\lambda_{ijt} = \frac{f(-J_{ijt})}{(1 - F(-J_{ijt}))} , \qquad (A6.3)$$

where f and F are, respectively, the density and cumulative standard normal distribution function. Then, the sample is restricted to observations for which $NS/TS>0$, and a usual OLS regression is run, in which the estimated correction variable, λ, is included:

---

estimation procedures would be complex. In the vector Z, however, a lot of characteristics for individual firms as well as countries are included which partly may capture fixed effects.

$$\frac{NS_{ijt}}{TS_{it}} = \gamma_0 + Z'\gamma_1 + \sigma\tilde{\lambda}_{ijt} + v_{ijt} \, . \tag{A6.4}$$

The estimated γ's are here the marginal effects of the explanatory variables on overseas production.[86] Since Heckman's lambda is included, this OLS equation will yield consistent parameter estimates. The estimated standard errors will, however, be inefficient since we use the estimated rather than the actual value of λ. A White (1980) correction for heteroscedasticity is therefore required in order to obtain efficient standard errors of the estimated parameters. The residuals in equation 6.4 are then assumed to have the properties $v \sim N(0, \sigma_v^2)$, $E(v_{hjt}v_{ijt})=0$ for $h \neq i$ and $E(v_{ijt}v_{ikt})=0$ for $j \neq k$, but, similar to ϵ, $E(v_{ijs}v_{ijt}) \neq 0$ for $s \neq t$.

The advantage of applying SBCR as compared to the Tobit method can be summarized as follows: (1) The marginal and probability effects are separable and will *not* necessarily be equal in SBCR, whereas in the case of Tobit these two sets of effects are treated as identical; (2) The Tobit method provides a continuous distribution of the predicted values of the dependent variable. The SBCR method allows the first positive predicted observation to "jump" from zero to a high positive value.

---

[86] It should be noted that the probit and corrected OLS equations include the same explanatory variables in the vector Z. A possible practical problem is then multicollinearity between Z and λ. There is no theoretical basis that such problems must arise, however, since the latter variable is a *non-linear* combination of Z while OLS is a *linear* estimation technique. By excluding any of the firm variables in the OLS equation, it was verified that the results for the remaining parameter estimates were robust.

Chapter 7

CONCLUSION

7.1 Introduction

The main objective of this book has been to empirically trace the presence of certain key elements attributed to the "new economy". In particular, we have tried to shed light on the role of knowledge accumulation, size and network—or cluster—production in the performance of firms, in view of the increased internationalization and technological progress that have characterized the last decades. To achieve this end, we conducted a number of empirical studies that analyze different aspects of these issues with a focus on firms' profitability and international competitiveness. In addition, we compared the regulatory framework and cluster dynamics between the U.S.and Europe, with emphasis on Sweden. Finally, we examined how the prevalence of a support system of large and small firms in a region affect the locational decisions of multinational firms. The main results were summarized in the introduction. In the following section, we briefly recapitulate some of the findings and also discuss avenues for future research and the ensuing policy implications. Even though the analysis in the book primarily referred to data from Sweden, we believe that the results can be generalized to other countries and regions as well.

We commenced by reviewing the Swedish SME sector and the major trends that have characterized SMEs internationally as well as within Sweden. We found that most countries have seen a trendwise shift in production toward smaller firms; however, this shift seems to be less notable in Sweden. In addition to this general picture, we also presented a detailed data set on Swedish firms that contained information on the stock of knowledge within the firms. These stocks include investments in R&D, marketing, education and software. The data set was then used in some of the following empirical analyses.

In Chapter 3, the relationship between knowledge capital, size and profitability was investigated. The concept of knowledge, and the measuring problems associated with knowledge factors, was first discussed. From the empirical analyses, we concluded that the knowledge endowment of firms was positively associated with the rate of profitability; however, we found that firm size had no such impact on profitability.

In Chapter 4, we began by testing whether sunk costs in firm-specific knowledge assets were increasing with firm size. According to one strand of the literature, sunk costs are endogenous in market size. That suggests that firms producing similar products can be expected to have approximately the same relative sunk cost in knowledge assets, measured, for instance, as knowledge assets per employee. A weak positive relationship was also found to exist between size and relative knowledge endowments, albeit at a decreasing rate. Thus, the implemented data set tended to reject the endogeneity hypothesis. Still, the relationship between knowledge assets and firm size indicates that, after a certain level of knowledge accumulation was reached, diseconomies of scale in handling knowledge appear. This is likely to be related to the special character of knowledge, making it even harder to monitor, and to exploit, than many other assets within the firm. This result is important since it validates the assumption of decreasing return to knowledge investment on the firm level, which is often made in, for instance, growth theory.

Furthermore, the accumulation of knowledge appeared as a prerequisite for gaining international competitiveness, measured as export intensity. In this case, size also plays an important role. In other words, larger firms have a higher propensity to export part of their production, which mirrors the necessity to exploit economies of scale. We conclude that, even though the accumulation of knowledge is a crucial determinant of firms' internationalization and profitability, firms of different sizes have different abilities and perform different tasks in industrial production.

We proceeded with a comparative study on cluster dynamics (Chapter 5) in Europe, with emphasis on Sweden, and in the U.S. We discussed how flexibility in all dimensions is necessary for firms engaged in the new economy. High risks and short payoff times necessitate that firms operate in a flexible environment. We also demonstrated how tax wedges and regulations may hinder the development of a sophisticated venture capital market. A well-developed venture capital ondustry is the key to transforming entrepreneurial ideas into commercialized products and services.

The final analytical chapter examined whether network factors influence the locational decisions of large firms; that is, in Chapter 6 we discussed whether regions or countries that are dense with similar production to that of the investing firm were preferred investment locational sites. When we controlled for market size, exports, factor endowments, and a number of firm-specific variables, the results did indeed indicate such a positive relationship. However, it was confined to a sector categorized as "high-tech," where the categorization was based on R&D intensity. Hence, a prevalence of similar production seems to increase the attractiveness of a region for high-tech production. We interpreted this association to be related to the fact that the investing firm then has access to suppliers of goods and skills—a network—which is essential for its production. Consequently, both input-output linkages and knowledge spillovers seem to influence the locational pattern of large firms.

7.2 Policy Implications and Future Research

From a policy perspective, the applied microeconomic analysis conducted in this book stresses the importance of knowledge and flexibility. First, a higher endowment of knowledge was shown to have a positive impact on profitability. If we believe that higher profitability leads to more investment and production of goods with a high value-added content, then the welfare implications are obvious. Such production tends to increase demand for skilled, often well paid, labor. In fact, knowledge-based economic operations have also been shown to generate new employment opportunities, paralleled by wage increases. Hence, there seems to be a way around the generally perceived trade-off between higher employment and low wages, as illustrated by the development in Silicon Valley, the research triangle in North Carolina, and the Cambridge area in the United Kingdom (Audretsch and Thurik, 1999). It was also demonstrated in the preceding analysis that the prime source of firms' knowledge endowment is the composition of their labor force.

Second, we concluded that the international competitiveness of firms is increasing in their knowledge endowments, and that knowledge-intensive firms tend to direct investments to regions and countries that have similar production. This suggests that economic policy must be geared to sustain and improve a country's knowledge base. Hence, the education system must meet the requirements demanded by the commercial sector, and university research must be internationally competitive. But it also suggests that the institutions of a country must be designed such that interactions and communication (bridging) are allowed and stimulated between small and large firms, service and manufacturing industries, universities and firms, and so forth. Bridging has implications for the regulatory framework, particularly for start-ups of new firms, the design of the tax system, and the labor market. In fact, it involves a whole range of areas related to the overall institutional setting in a country, such as proprietary rules, openness, and so on. If a country fails in this respect, it may find that investments—particularly of large firms—are concentrated in other regions and countries, where, after a while, agglomeration forces may further increase the attractiveness of such regions. In the long run, this may show up in divergent growth rates across regions and countries, with clear welfare effects. As shown by Carree and Thurik (1999), downsizing and a large share of smaller firms seem to be positively correlated with growth.

As demonstrated in the preceding discussion, flexibility is a key ingredient in industries characterized by rapid technological progress, high risks and short pay-off periods. To promote start-ups and growth of firms based in the new economy, the labor market plays a critical role in most European countries. Yet, reforms in the labor market are not enough. New contract forms emphasize the importance of coordinating such reforms with reforms related to the tax structure. That goes for individual employees, partly paid in stock options, as well as for providers of venture capital. The latter play a crucial role in transforming new ideas into commercial products. The higher risks associated with these investments must be paralleled by a similarly high return on successful investments.

An important field for future research is in more closely identifying the mechanism behind agglomeration, or cluster, economies, and the dynamics taking place in these clusters. Several studies suggest an increased role for SMEs in R&D, where large firms have begun to outsource activities that used to be considered strategically important to preserve within the firm. As the barriers to trade and investment continue to decrease, paralleled by falling trade costs and increased use of IT, we can expect the forces behind agglomeration to increase in the future.

How new is the new economy and how important has knowledge capital actually become? In the preceding analysis, some of the data was collected in the early 1990s, and obviously knowledge then was crucial for profitability and international competitiveness at the firm level. It is not likely to fade away: Marshall claimed as early as 1879 that "knowledge is the most prominent engine of growth" (Marshall, 1879), a view shared by numerous economists since then. Perhaps more interesting is how large the knowledge-based sector has grown. According to the OECD, in applying a relatively wide definition of knowledge-based industries, these industries account for more than 50 percent of GDP in most industrialized countries. This is a considerable increase compared with the 1980s. Still, other studies, where traditional industries like television, radio, basic consumer electronics, and so forth have been deducted to obtain a more realistic picture of the knowledge-based sector in the new economy, conclude that the true figure is closer to 5 percent than it is to 50 percent of GDP, at least in the U.S. (The Economist, 1999). That may seem less impressive, but it means that this sector has surpassed the car industry and doubled in size in a decade. Other figures show that the IT investment share in the U.S. capital stock is about 10 percent, which happens to be close to the share the railroad had when it became important for growth and commerce about a century ago. Thus, it seems appropriate to take the signs of a knowledge-based new economy seriously.

Since knowledge tends to be "sticky", particularly the more tacit and complex it gets, there may be distinct first-mover advantages in knowledge-intensive industries. The obvious example is, of course, the Silicon Valley story. In addition, agglomeration and clusters tend to be particularly strong in new and knowledge-intensive industries (Kim, 1999). All knowledge-intensive production will not end up in the same place; rather, such production will be fragmented across regions and continents. Nonetheless, future growth and distribution of welfare may be trapped along different paths across countries. Thus, the future largely looms in relation to the capabilities of politicians to promote a knowledge-dense and flexible environment conducive for economic activities in the new economy.

LITERATURE

Audretsch, D. and Thurik R. (eds.), 1999, *Innovation, Industry Employment, and Evolution*, Cambridge University Press, Cambridge.
Carree, M. and R. Thurik, 1999, "Industrial Structure and Economic Growth", in Audretsch, D. and Thurik, R. (eds.), 1999, *Innovation, Industry Employment, and Evolution*, Cambridge University Press, Cambridge.
The Economist, 1999, "The New Economy. E-xaggeration", October 30th.
Kim, S., 1999, "Urban Development in the United States, 1690-1990", *NBER WP*, No. 7120, May.
Marshall, A., 1890, *The Principles of Economics*, MacMillan, London.

INDEX

Economics of Science, Technology and Innovation

18. J. S. Metcalfe and I. Miles (eds.):
    Innovation Systems in the Service Economy:
    Measurement and Case Study Analysis   ISBN 0-7923-7730-3
19. R. Svensson:
    Success Strategies and Knowledge Transfer in
    Cross-Border Consulting Operations   ISBN 0-7923-7776-1
20. P. Braunerhjelm:
    Knowledge Capital and the "New Economy":
    Firm Size, Performance and Network Production   ISBN 0-7923-7801-6

KLUWER ACADEMIC PUBLISHERS — BOSTON / DORDRECHT / LONDON